M000202329

10 WEEK BIBLE

JOHN

10 Week Books
10WeekBooks.com

JOHN: A 10 WEEK BIBLE STUDY

ISBN: 0-9889195-9-1
ISBN-13: 978-0-9889195-9-4

Cover: Healing The Man Born Blind, El Greco - Public Domain

10WeekBooks.com

For Ella

You are forever loved by your parents and by God. May He continually bless you with His showering love and may you fall in love with Him and His Word more and more through your life.

CONTENTS

ABOUT THE
10 WEEK BIBLE STUDY

A Bible study's shelf life isn't much more than 10 weeks. Even a great one. This isn't McDonald's. Any more than 10 weeks and you've got a stale, moldy study.

It's hard to get people to stay engaged with any one topic for longer than 10 weeks. There are natural life cycles that prevent people from engaging any longer than that: children's school, holidays, work trips, sickness and vacations all break up our year and keep us from focusing on anything for much longer. How often has an unwelcome disruption wrecked your 4-week string of good workouts?

People are often intimidated by leading a Bible study. They do not feel they have the Bible knowledge or theological training to lead others to a deeper knowledge of God. Nothing could be farther from the truth. The Holy Spirit and a willing person, in that order, are all you need to have a great Bible study where people's lives are brought closer to God.

But people still struggle. It is that whole "flesh is weak" thing.

THE 10 WEEK BIBLE DISTINCTIVES

This Bible study will overcome most peoples' problems in four distinct ways:

10 Weeks – no mold here!

Format – no lesson plans needed!

Repetition – the key to learning anything well!

Commentary – background helps built right in!

That's all there is to it. You've got everything you need for a successful Bible study right here. So why is that important?

There is great need.

There are so many people in need of discipleship and this little book is designed to take away any insecurities you may have about leading a Bible study. Now, go out and find a group of people who need more of the Lord!

But still, leading can be hard. Even the greatest leaders had to learn to lead somewhere, and since great leadership skills are learned through confidence, this study is ready-made to create confident leaders of tomorrow.

Through a consistent format everyone in the group can focus on the study itself instead of how the group should flow. No more awkward tension of having to take the snack tray out of the stragglers hands so you can get started.

If you make clear the format of the meeting on the front end, everyone will be able to march to the same drum and no energy is needed on logistics.. Here's how it works:

Scripture Reading Out Loud

We read out loud because we do not always know how well people can read. Do not assume everyone in your group can read or read well. You would be surprised who cannot and you do not want them to feel uncomfortable, so do not ever ask someone to read, let them volunteer.

Study Questions

These are some basic questions to get discussion going for the chapter. If you spend the entire time on questions one and two; no problem! This book is a guide to get people excited about God's Word.

Assignments & Closing Prayer

Make a point to remind everyone each week that this study hinges on them reading the entire book each week between studies. They get out of the study what they put into it. Pray that God will enlighten each heart to apply what they learn and bless everyone as they go.

The Theory

Many people are relatively unfamiliar with the Bible and that intimidates them from participating in group Bible studies. This book will guide you into a deeper knowledge in two very important ways: 1) Macro and 2) Micro knowledge.

Micro knowledge is what is gained through most Bible studies. That's when you break apart some part of scripture in detail and try to apply it to your life. But with an hour a week and 10 weeks before people drift away into that moldy oblivion, that doesn't leave you with a broad base of information from any book. That's where the Macro part of the 10 Week Bible Study comes in.

Macro study is where you gain an good overview of the book, enhancing your overall Biblical literacy. Knowing the Bible—lots of it—is daunting to a lot of people. Many have tried to read the One Year Bible only to lay it down around Psalms or Isaiah. What the 10 Week Bible Study does is help you increase your Biblical literacy one book at a time.

That is accomplished by weekly reading. This is Repetition. We read the whole book every single week during our own quiet time. Depending on your reading speed, that amounts to between 10 and 20 minutes a day of reading—not a huge commitment. But what you will have at the end of 10 weeks IS HUGE: you will have read the book 10 times and studied each chapter in detail!

The important thing when reading the book through each week is not to stop and get hung up on details you don't understand. There's an important concept at work here that many people don't realize and they give up on scripture before they have to.

I call it the MEDITATION PRINCIPLE.

The more you read the Word, the more you have it in your mind throughout the week. The more it's in your mind, the more you'll meditate on it. The more you meditate on it, the more the Holy Spirit will give you enlightenment into it. The more Holy Spirit enlightenment you have, the better you'll understand it and the more you'll be able to apply it to your life.

David recognized this and it's why the entire book of Psalms starts this way:

¹Blessed is the man
who does not walk in the counsel of the wicked
or stand in the way of sinners
or sit in the seat of mockers.
²But his delight is in the law of the Lord,
and on his law he meditates day and night.
³He is like a tree planted by streams of water,
which yields its fruit in season
and whose leaf does not wither.
Whatever he does prospers.

Psalm 1:1-3

When we read the same book in a repetitive manner, it forces us to meditate on it. After reading a book of the Bible 10 times you'll catch yourself asking God questions about it even when you didn't mean to. David knew the power of God's Word was in his ability to fill his own heart with it. I've been personally changed by this and I know it brings the Bible alive in a way I'd never thought possible before.

THE HELP

Because so many questions can come up during a Bible study, it's always helpful to have a little guidance. There's no better guidance than the Holy Spirit, but having a commentary sure can help sometimes. That's why we have them.

The commentary provided will give you some background, biographical and historical context to better understand what you're reading. The Bible is an amazing book. Its information is always timeless, but it was written with definite cultural and historical understandings in mind. Without commentaries it is sometimes impossible to get the whole picture.

This commentary is not designed to replace your study of scripture, but simply to speed up your comprehension of it. Make sure that you read each passage directly from scripture before engaging with the commentary.

INTRODUCTION TO JOHN

TRULY UNIQUE

John is a book of definites and a book of paradoxes. It is a book of sureties and a book of questions. It will help you better understand the deity of Jesus, His intentions and His great love and it will cause you question just as many things that you thought you knew. John is a book that is truly unique in the New Testament and the entire canon of scripture itself.

John stands alone among the gospels as the most unique of the four. It tells different stories, and the ones it shares with other gospels, it tells differently. It is a fascinating study on the life, ministry and person of Jesus and it is often the book of the Bible new Christians and non-Christians are instructed to read first, not because it is the easiest to understand, but because it is the one that may cause you to ask the most questions.

John poses questions to us in all the right ways. It is not a book that will give us questions that cause doubt, it is a book that gives us questions to ask that will encourage us and cause us to seek God on a deeper level. There are many things John tells us we know for sure and many things where he hints at the apparent paradoxes he himself introduces: not paradoxes of apparent conflict of scripture, but the paradoxes brought up by God becoming a man.

MORE QUESTIONS

How can God be unseeable yet we see Him in Jesus? How can God not judge mankind while judging them all at the same time? How can Jesus be with God and be God? These are some of the questions John raises on purpose, for a purpose.

Studying John should not leave us with more answers, but with more questions. The right kinds of questions. The ones where we run to God to find the answers as opposed to running away from Him for understanding. John finishes his book with a fascinating statement that further illustrates this point:

> *Jesus did many other things as well. If every one of them were written down, I suppose that even the whole world would not have room for the books that would be written.*

> *John 21:25*

John was not intending to undertake a full account of Jesus' life in his gospel. He knew that would be impossible. He had a point for writing his book and it was to call attention to the glory, majesty and wonder that is Jesus Christ. We find that he probably knew Jesus better than anyone on earth, and John himself was left with more wonder than knowledge, more questions than answers. This same John, the John who rested upon Jesus' chest at the last supper, the one who should have known Jesus fully, was the same John given the narrative in the book of Revelation. In that book, John is again amazed and intrigued by the person he meets, the Jesus he should have already known so well.

John's gospel is not primarily about getting to know Jesus as a man, but getting to know that a man named Jesus was God. John makes that an unmistakable fact in the opening lines of his gospel, immediately equating Jesus with God Himself and also with the very written Words of God, the Old Testament. "In the beginning, the Word was with God, and the Word was God."

Jesus was not a witness to creation. He was not just a part of it. Jesus was the creator Himself. How exactly the Trinity works, or how God the Father, Jesus the Son and the Holy Spirit differ, differentiate or delineate is beyond the scope of understanding, but Jesus the Son was nonetheless there in the beginning and an active participant in it.

John, in his gospel, is not trying to simply introduce you to Jesus, he wants you to share his appreciation, wonder, awe and love for Him. John is sometimes called The Evangelist because his gospel, above all, is not an account of Jesus' life, but a pitch to share in what he knows. The heart of evangelism is to share the good thing that you have found with others. We naturally evangelize our friends and family for products and services that we find especially useful. In this book, John is evangelizing the person he has found to be of greatest value in his life, one whom he can easily share with others.

John does not necessarily list all of his stories in chronological order. Some of the stories would seem to be out of place when viewed in light of the other three gospels, but John never makes an assertion that he is recounting things entirely chronologically; that would be our assumption.

AUTHORSHIP

The title in your Bible is John, but authorship is never mentioned. We are able to easily deduce that our author is John, the Apostle of the Lamb, one of the twelve. As with many other things in his gospel, John hints at himself being the author without ever coming right out and saying it.

Six times John uses a phrase to describe a certain disciple of Jesus, "the disciple Jesus loved." We understand that this is John himself because of how John concludes his gospel. In John 21:20-24, he tells the story of Jesus prophesying Peter's future death on a cross. After receiving the disturbing news, Peter looks at this disciple whom Jesus loved and asked, "what about him?" Jesus responded that if He wanted that disciple to live forever, what was it to Peter? That disciple goes on to say that it was he who wrote this book (21:24).

We know this to be John because Jesus references this same disciple as the one whom He gave charge of His mother (19:26-27). Church history tells us that this was John the Apostle of the Lamb (one of the twelve) and that eventually they moved to Ephesus before John was ultimately exiled to the Island of Patmos where he had his vision of the book of Revelation.

Some people have been offended at the idea of Jesus loving one disciple over the others, but this may not be what John meant when he said this. Some have said it could be John saying this phrase "tongue-in-cheek" as a joke with the other apostles or that it was even John's declaration of his own love for Jesus. John was, after all, a hardened fisherman, the one who asked Jesus to call down fire on others (Luke 9:54). He was a tough man who was called a "son of thunder," (Mark 3:17) so it was a big step for John to associate himself with something so weak and tender as being the disciple that Jesus loved; the one who "leaned upon Jesus' breast."

This association would be so far from the normal character of a rough fisherman, it may say much more about who John assumed himself to become after having known Jesus than how Jesus felt about John. We know that God does not show favoritism (Romans 2:11, Acts 10:34), so it could have also been the title John gave himself as the caretaker of Jesus' mother, someone who obviously would have been especially close to Jesus' heart. In the end, we do not know exactly why John referred to himself this way, only that we are sure he did.

THE RUMOR OF JOHN

Just before the end of the book, John references Jesus' curious words about him "remaining until I return" to make a point. Church history tells us that John was to be martyred like every other of the twelve Apostles of the Lamb were, except that when the authorities tried to kill him, it didn't work. The story goes (an extra-biblical account) that John was to be killed by being thrown into a large vat of boiling oil. This would have been an excruciatingly painful death, one where John's outsides would melt away before his insides were overcome. When he was thrown in the vat of oil, he simply sat there, unharmed. Those looking on were so taken aback, and so afraid of John after that, they never tried to kill him again, but only exiled him to the Island of Patmos to shut him up.

How much of the story is true we do not know, but we know that John was well aware that people had heard of it and felt it necessary to address it by saying Jesus didn't literally tell Peter that John wouldn't die (21:23). We know that John did eventually die, but he was the one apostle of the twelve who was not martyred.

OUTLINE OF JOHN

Introduction & Purpose 1:1-18

Miracles, Signs and Confrontations 1:19-12:50

Jesus' teachings 13-17

Jesus' Crucifixion & Resurrection 18-20

Conclusion 21

JOHN IN 10 WEEKS

JOHN 1-2

STUDY QUESTIONS

1. Why would the world not receive the light? If you had been living then, do you think you would have accepted Jesus? Why?

2. Who is Elijah?

   Who is the Prophet?

   Who is the Messiah?

3. Why did Jesus rename Simon?

4. Why would Nathanael say nothing good comes from Nazareth?

5. What is a paradox? Why do they make it more difficult to know about someone as opposed to actually knowing them?

What is a paradox about yourself that only those close to you would understand?

COMMENTARY NOTES

JOHN CHAPTER 1

THE BOOK OF PARADOXES

A paradox is a statement that seems contradictory because it contains two statements that are both true, but do not seem to be true at the same time. A paradox causes us to wrestle with what we know to be true. It forces us to reexamine what we believe and how we see the world, and if what we believe does not conform to the paradox, we must change our thinking.

John begins with a divine paradox that beckons us to evaluate our beliefs about God. He is going to challenge us before we have finished the first sentence of his gospel. John tells us that the Word was *with* God and the Word *was* God.

How can the Word be *with* someone and *be* that someone at the same time? It is this paradox that John prefaces his book with, and it won't be the last. In fact, John will fill his book throughout with paradoxes for us to wrestle with.

John is recommended as the book that new believers should start with when beginning to read the Bible, and for good reason. It is so masterfully written that it will instruct all further Bible study or it will undo a lifetime of Bible study that has resulted in man making a god of his own creation.

All too often that spirit of religion that has gripped mankind for centuries takes over in our lives and we choose to read the Bible in a way that suits us most conveniently.

John has made a point to keep us from that. His paradoxes will continually challenge our understanding of who God really is and how we understand Him and relate to Him.

If you are new to studying scripture, John is an excellent place to start because it will force you to go to the true Author for help. If you have studied scripture for decades, John will force you to deal with every wayward thought about God you have ever placed in the recesses of your mind.

John does not want us to serve a god of our own choosing, but he wants to introduce us to the One and True God, as He really is. His book is not one of information about Jesus, but an invitation to know Jesus.

THE DIVINE PARADOX
1:1-5

Getting back to John's first paradox, how can the Word, whom we will soon find out is Jesus Himself, be with God and be God at the same time? I do not think of being myself and being with myself at the same time. How is it that Jesus is God and is with God?

John confronts us with the difficult nature of the Trinity in the first words of his book. As we will see throughout this book, John's primary purpose is to show that the Messiah is both a man and God at the same time. While this may seem a normal proposition for seasoned believers and people who have spent a lifetime in modern Western Christianity, this was sacrilege to first century Jews.

The notion that the Messiah could be one with God wasn't just a foreign idea to most of John's readers, to them it was the very blasphemy they would crucify Jesus for.

John moves on to double-down on his premise that Jesus is God in the flesh. He tells his readers that this Word was the creator of all things and that without Him nothing was made. Jews would have believed that God alone created all things, but John tells us that it was actually Jesus who had the task of creation. We see this repeated in John's book of Revelation:

> Whenever the living creatures give glory, honor and thanks to him who sits on the throne and who lives for ever and ever, the twenty-four elders fall down before him who sits on the throne and worship him who lives for ever and ever. They lay their crowns before the throne and say:
>
> "You are worthy, our Lord and God,
>
> to receive glory and honor and power,
>
> for you created all things,
>
> and by your will they were created
>
> and have their being."
>
> *Revelation 4:9-11*

Again in Revelation 5 we see that Jesus is the one standing in the center of the throne with His Father:

> Then I saw a Lamb, looking as if it had been slain, standing at the center of the throne, encircled by the four living creatures and the elders.
>
> *Revelation 5:6*

Somehow we are to understand that Jesus and God are one and that at the same time they are somehow separate. This is the trouble of the Trinity. This is one of the most difficult truths about God to comprehend, one that has racked the minds of men throughout history. So challenging is this doctrine that the Jews completely reject it and Muslims have inscribed an argument against it as the primary message on the Dome of the Rock in Jerusalem.

Paul told us that this message of the gospel would be seen as foolishness to Gentiles and a stumbling block to Jews (1 Corinthians 1:23). This is the concept that John begins his book with because he has no desire for us to know *about* Jesus. He wants us to know Him personally. We will only know Him personally if we choose to move past the seeming contradictions of His nature and ask Him directly about them.

A MAN SENT FROM GOD
1:6-8

John the author of this book quickly introduces us to another man named John. He tells us that John came to tell us about a light. What light? The One True Light that shines on the darkness of sin. The Light that leads us out of darkness. Our author tells us that John was not that light, but that he testified of that light. The light that causes those in darkness to come out of it or reject it.

LIFE THAT IS LIGHT
1:9-14

It is for this rejection of the light that the world could not accept the very light that had come into their darkness. What a tragic statement on the state of the human heart! Jesus is the life we need and He is the light that will shine into our darkness, but because we are offended by these kinds of seeming contradictions, we refuse Him.

People inherently self-justify themselves. Who is bad? Other people. Who are true sinners? Other people. Deep down, we are never really the problem. Our hearts seek to find a way out so that we can be self-righteous and self-justified. We are not as bad as other people, so we must be okay, or so our hearts deceive us to believe.

God became a man and walked among mankind and they did not recognize Him nor receive Him. What is it that would make us different today than in Jesus' day? How can we accept the light that has come into this world?

John does not want us to be comfortable with our current understanding of God and he uses the first few words of his book to let us know that it needs adjustment. The fact that the light came into the world and the world could not recognize it should send shivers down our spines. How could this be? What was it in the heart of mankind that they would miss the very Messiah so long hoped for? What is it inside us that would cause us to do the same?

THOSE WHO DID RECEIVE
1:15-17

Not everyone chose to reject the light. To those who chose to accept that light that came into the world was given the honor of becoming a child of God. What makes that difference, though? How can we be one who accepts that light versus one who rejects it?

The paradoxes and challenges John gives us in his book are not intended to obscure the nature of Jesus, but to reveal it. John does not want us to read his book and continue on in our complacent and incorrect understanding of who God is. He wants to tear down every wrong belief about God that would keep us from accepting that light.

John's gospel will illustrate over and over again the things that hinder us from knowing God and that keep us from Him. All too often it is our own self-justification that causes us to refuse that light. We choose our own darkness instead of the light that could free us from our chains.

NO ONE HAS SEEN GOD
1:18

John quickly moves into his next paradox. We are told that we have seen the Word (Jesus) and beheld His glory. He began by telling us that that Word was God Himself. Now John goes on to say that no one has ever seen God except the Son. How is it that they saw Jesus face to face but no one had ever seen God? If Jesus was God, hadn't they seen Him?

How can we both look upon God and at the same time He be hidden from our view? These are the kinds of questions that John poses to us that will drive us mad if we try to answer them ourselves. But that is not his goal.

John longs for us to go to the author of these paradoxes Himself to find our answers. In this way, John is not trying to teach us about Jesus as much as he is trying to introduce us to Jesus. John will create more mysteries about God that cannot be answered than definitive answers about Him. That is not to say that we cannot know God, but that John doesn't want us to know Him by studying his book. John wants us to know God because we have become acquainted with Him personally.

JOHN THE BAPTIST
1:19-28

Our author moves quickly back to John the Baptist who was asked who he was. This introduces some themes found in our book that probably will be foreign to most modern Gentile readers.

The leaders of the Jews asked John if he was the Messiah, Elijah or the Prophet. All three of the questions carry a very different connotation to ancient Jews than to modern readers and they carry deep meaning we must pause to consider before moving on.

In the ancient Jewish understanding, the Messiah was a man who was going to come and militarily restore the nation of Israel back to God's people, then go on to conquer and subdue all nations to worship the One True God and be subject to Israel and the Messiah's rulership. He, in their understanding, could not be a man because earth is God's footstool (Isaiah 66:1), and God Himself could not be bothered to stoop to such lowly levels.

Asking John if he was Elijah comes from two places. In the book of Kings, we find that Elijah somehow did not die but was swept up to heaven in a chariot of fire. Then in Malachi 4:5-6, the Hebrew Bible's final words, God tells His people that He will send Elijah to reunite them, father to son and son to father, before the coming of the day of the Lord.

Asking if John was the Prophet refers to Moses' prophecy that God would raise up a man like himself, and to him Israel must obey every word.

The Lord your God will raise up for you a prophet like me from among you, from your fellow Israelites. You must listen to him. For this is what you asked of the Lord your God at Horeb on the day of the as-

sembly when you said, "Let us not hear the voice of the Lord our God nor see this great fire anymore, or we will die."

The Lord said to me: "What they say is good. I will raise up for them a prophet like you from among their fellow Israelites, and I will put my words in his mouth. He will tell them everything I command him. I myself will call to account anyone who does not listen to my words that the prophet speaks in my name.

Deuteronomy 18:15-19

The Jews were awaiting this Prophet to come and explain everything they did not understand.

They pressed John and asked him to explain, from scripture, who he thought he was. John was speaking with great authority, authority they themselves had not granted him, and they wanted to know under what presumption he spoke as he did.

John answered them that he was the prophesied voice in Isaiah 40:3 who would prepare the way for the Messiah. That confused the Jewish leaders because they didn't understand what business he had baptizing people if he was just a messenger and not one with the authority of the Prophet, Messiah or Elijah.

John told them that his baptism was that of preparation and not of completion. It was a foreshadowing of the One who would come and baptize the earth with the Holy Spirit.

I DID NOT KNOW HIM
1:29-34

The next day John sees Jesus and he proclaims that He is the Chosen One from God. He proclaims a phrase that John our author will make his own from here on out. "Look, the Lamb of God, who takes away the sin of the world."

John the Baptist then goes on to say that he did not know Jesus. We know from Matthew and Luke that John and Jesus were cousins, so what did John mean when he said he did not know Jesus? John was told by God that he would see the Spirit come down on a man and remain, and that would be the Messiah. John saw this when he baptized Jesus, a fact that our author leaves out of his gospel. John testified that the prophetic word he had been told was fulfilled with Jesus.

John knew Jesus in the sense that they were family, but he did not know Jesus in the sense that He truly came from a place he had not been. John the Baptist was a man, and he was testifying to the fact that Jesus was actually from somewhere beyond this earth.

THE FIRST DISCIPLES
1:35-50

The following day we see that Andrew and another unnamed disciple leave John the Baptist and begin following Jesus. It may be that he is unnamed because John himself is that disciple who was a fellow fisherman with Andrew and Peter. John is often coy about those details in his book, but the important fact here is that Andrew went and got his brother, Simon to come and meet Jesus. Jesus meets him and immediately changes his name forevermore to Peter (literally, "a rock").

The following day Jesus met Philip and invited him to come along. Philip immediately goes and finds Nathanael sitting under a tree and tells him to come meet the Messiah from Nazareth.

Nathanael exclaims that nothing good can come from Nazareth. Many have seen this as a slight against a backwards fishing village of some sort, but that is not what Nathanael meant. We will see this phrase repeated in a similar way throughout John's gospel. It has to do with the fact that there are no Old Testament prophesies about Nazareth, and certainly none about the Messiah being from there.

Philip persisted with Nathanael and encouraged him to come meet Jesus anyway. When Nathanael met Jesus, He told him he had seen Nathanael sitting under the tree and the exchange between he and Philip. Philip knew that no one could possibly have seen that unless God had shown them. For that reason he decided to follow Jesus.

Jesus then gives him a most amazing promise. He promises that Nathanael will see exactly the same thing that Jacob, father Israel, had seen at Bethel (Genesis 28:10-19).

JOHN CHAPTER 2

THE FIRST MIRACLE
2:1-12

After our brief introductions, John moves on to the first miracle of Jesus at a wedding in Cana. Jesus was there with His mother and brothers and the host of the wedding ran out of wine.

This was a major offense in that day, as it meant that the fun would soon come to an end. The host had not planned correctly and everyone would sober up. Most people at weddings were probably not punch drunk, but they probably had enough of a buzz on to keep the good times rolling.

The conversation between Mary and Jesus is most interesting and has dramatic implications. Mary either had compassion on the host or was irritated with him, but she enlists Jesus against His will to do something about the matter. Her confidence in Jesus' abilities is telling of His activity in private with His family.

Jesus told Mary that His hour hadn't yet come, presumably to be revealed to outsiders. But at her insistence, He changed the water to wine anyway. It begs the question of whether or not Mary, a human, changed God's plans to reveal Himself.

We know from the entirety of scripture that God's mind is not changed by man, but that He also loves people and desires partnership with them. Exactly what happened here remains a mystery, but Jesus certainly uses the opportunity to show the world who He is and that what God saves for the end is certainly the best.

JESUS' ZEAL
2:13-17

The next story John tells us leaves us with some questions about the timing of his narrative. In other gospels, this story is told later in Jesus' ministry. It could be that others omit this happening on more than one occasion, or John may not be telling his stories in strictly chronological order. Whatever is the case, we see a window into Jesus' nature.

When Jesus found the merchants in the Temple courts, He became angry and started beating them, flipping over tables and driving them out. In other gospel accounts, He seems to even accuse them of ripping off the people buying from them.

In those days, if you were unable or too poor to bring a sacrifice with you, you could purchase the required sacrifices there. It seems that the merchants cared nothing for the holiness of the place and were even using poor out-of-towners' needs to swindle them.

The scene must have been a bit awkward and embarrassing for Jesus' disciples. John tells us that the disciples at some point remembered that Jesus' zeal for His house would consume Him as it is written in Psalm 69:9.

AUTHORITY
2:18-25

The Jewish leaders asked Jesus a question that would become a staple for them: under whose authority do you do these things? Jesus' answer is very odd. He doesn't directly tell them by whose authority He cleared the Temple, but responded by prophesying about His death and resurrection.

The disciples were just as confused by Jesus' statement as the Jewish leaders were, but John tells us that after Jesus had risen from the dead they remembered these critical words spoken years earlier.

Jesus went on to do miracles in Jerusalem and people followed Him, but He would not "entrust" Himself to them. John is telling us that Jesus did not use these people to try and further His ministry or platform. He could have leveraged their faith for fame and fortune, but Jesus knew that

He had authority over all and did not need the testimony from anyone.

One point John will make over and over again in this book is that Jesus has authority not granted by anyone but God. The issue of authority will be a recurring feature of John's Gospel.

Don't forget to read John this week!
READ IT | KNOW IT | LIVE IT
For the word of God is living and active. Sharper than any double-edged sword, it penetrates even to dividing soul and spirit, joints and marrow; it judges the thoughts and attitudes of the heart. (Hebrews 4:12)

JOHN 3-4

STUDY QUESTIONS

1. How can John want to become less while Jesus becomes more? How can we choose to accept what God has given us instead of being in competition with those around us?

2. Who was Nicodemus? Why did he come to Jesus at night?

3. What does it mean to be born again?

4. Why does wrath remain on those who reject Jesus? Whose wrath is is?

5. What does it mean to worship in "spirit and truth?"

6. Why does Jesus explain clearly to the woman at the well that He is the Messiah, yet He speaks so mysteriously to everyone else?

7. Why does John mention the saying about a prophet not being accepted in his own country?

8. Why does Jesus respond so harshly to a father desperate to have his son healed?

COMMENTARY NOTES

JOHN CHAPTER 3

NICODEMUS
3:1-9

Nicodemus was part of the Sanhedrin (the 71 ruling counselors of Israel). In the exchange with Jesus, He calls Nicodemus "Israel's teacher" in a rather negative connotation. The Pharisees had established a very official way of becoming a teacher and leader. They required anyone to go through them to receive teaching, training and certification. They were the gatekeepers of who could teach and what could be taught. They made sure that no one taught unapproved things.

Jesus was not from their ranks and it ruffled their feathers because He had not received His authority from them. Our church world has much the same system today. We have denominational seminaries today and anyone who doesn't come through approved channels is not generally received well by those inside. The notion of having gatekeepers is not inherently bad, but the idea that we can effectively manage the teachings that come from God are.

We, who are here for a short time and then dead and gone cannot be the true gatekeepers of truths that are thousands of years old. Only the Holy Spirit is good enough to manage what is taught and how, and He has been very effective at maintaining the church for nearly two thousand years now. Divisions, heresies, fights, apostasies and every other problem has been survived by the church for one reason alone: God is good.

People are still being saved today by Jesus not because we have good systems in place to maintain doctrine, but because the Holy Spirit is the active leader of the church. Again, that doesn't mean that we should just sit idly by during our lifetime when heresies and dangerous doctrines of demons persist, but we also must have faith that the Lord will raise up for us people whom we haven't approved of and might not even like.

Nicodemus was from this gatekeeper community, but was curious enough about Jesus to find out if He was the real deal. He came to Jesus at night so he wouldn't be seen by any of his counterparts on the Sanhedrin or reported to them by someone who recognized him. He would eventually stand up for Jesus, albeit unsuccessfully, when He was on trial in absentia before the Sanhedrin.

LIFTED UP
3:10-15

Jesus told Nicodemus that He must be lifted up just like Moses lifted up the snake in the wilderness. Why would Jesus compare Himself to a snake?

When Israel was in the desert after their exodus from Egypt, a plague of poisonous snakes broke out and began killing Israelites. God told Moses to make an image of a snake and put it on a pole and raise it up high enough for everyone to see. When they would look at it after being bitten by a snake, the Lord would heal them. By gazing on the snake, the very object of scorn that had created their situation, God would use to heal them (Numbers 21:4-9).

Jesus, in the same way was raised up on a cross, one of the most heinous and scornful ways to die in human history. The Law proclaimed a curse on anyone who died on a pole (tree) in Deuteronomy 21:23. In that way, Jesus became the object of our salvation by hanging on an object of scorn. He took the curse of sin away from us by becoming that very curse for us.

JOHN 3:16
3:16-21

It is from this conversation with Nicodemus we gain the context of that famous verse, John 3:16. It is the most concise and easy to remember verse in scripture about God's love and eternal intention for us.

John also introduces a new paradox that will run throughout the book. He tells us that Jesus did not come into the world to condemn it, but to save it. We will see this statement seemingly be reversed back and forth several times in John's gospel. It will be important for us to understand the context and nature of God's salvation and condemnation as we read the book of John.

John concludes this statement about salvation and condemnation by returning to his metaphor from chapter one about light. Whoever loves the light will come into it and see and be saved, but whoever hates the light and loves darkness (sin) will reject the light and be condemned.

Most of the world rejected Jesus, and will continue to do so, not because it is a wise thing to do, but because people's sin causes them to reject Jesus, the light of the world.

I MUST BECOME LESS
3:22-36

We return again to John the Baptist for an important lesson about authority. John's disciples realized that Jesus was siphoning off all his followers. John responds with the true heart of servanthood and friendship.

"A person can receive only what is given them from heaven" (3:27). John understood that he was given a task to do. He could do nothing beyond what had been granted to him from heaven to do, and would not fight for anything more.

How often do we scratch and fight for more money, attention or favor? Money, attention and favor are not bad by themselves, but when we try to stretch out the grace given us by God we can make a mess of things. John understood who he was and what he was called to do. He understood that it was now time to fade into the background so that everyone would see Jesus instead.

John likened himself to a friend of the bridegroom. When we go to our friend's wedding, we are happy for them even though we are not the ones directly experiencing the new love of marriage. Our joy is being present to see the joy of new young love. John understood that he was not the bride or groom in his situation and he was happy anyway.

John concludes his sermon by saying that whoever believes in the Son (Jesus) will have eternal life. He also makes the opposite statement, that if anyone rejects Jesus, God's wrath will be on them. Here again we see this paradox that even though Jesus came to save the world, there will still be judgment and wrath.

Our author is not ready for us to reconcile these things just yet, but he wants us to know through these two stories that Jesus does love us with an eternal love and all we must do to receive it is to accept Him as our savior.

JOHN CHAPTER 4

SAMARIA

Jesus heard about the Pharisees' jealousy of Him now that He was getting quite famous, so He decided to leave their stomping grounds of Jerusalem and head north to Galilee. On His way to Galilee, He went through Samaria instead of going around it as was the normal route Jews would take.

The Jews bypassed Samaria for a couple of reasons. The ancient historian, Josephus, tells us that during that time there were constantly bandits along the roads and in the hill country of Samaria. Often, especially if traveling alone or unprotected, you would get robbed or even killed for whatever you had on you. Instead of traveling through the rugged hills of Samaria, Jews would go around it by way of the lower plains where no one could surprise them by jumping out from behind a rock.

Another reason Jews avoided Samaria was because of their prejudice against them. The Samaritans were the results of descendants of the northern tribes of Israel who had been defeated and carried away by the Assyrians. They had intermarried with Gentiles during their exile, which had been strictly prohibited by God. They also worshipped the false gods that had been established when Jeroboam set himself up as king when he rebelled against Solomon's son Rehoboam.

THE WOMAN AT THE WELL
4:1-15

John feels the need to point out that Jesus is traveling north because of a misunderstanding the Pharisees had about

Jesus baptizing. This will be the first of many, many misunderstandings that Jesus never sets out to correct the Pharisees on. He completely allows them to disrespect Him, discredit Him and deny Him.

Jesus sent His disciples into town to buy food, perhaps because He had already set up this encounter so that they would happen upon Him near the end of the conversation.

In those days, it was Jewish custom that no man would ever be caught talking to a woman alone, in public or not. This was especially bad practice for Jesus, since He was considered a Rabbi now to be talking to a woman, let alone a Samaritan woman. He was breaking all kinds of rules, but they were all rules designed to make the Rabbis look more "holier-than-thou" than your average Jew.

So bad was how women were looked down upon back then that a woman who sat alone on a road was to be assumed a witch or prostitute. If two women sat alone, it was "known" that they were witches. That is the context that this woman was approached by Jesus.

When Jesus asked the woman for a drink, she immediately recognized Him as a Jew, and perhaps as a Rabbi from how He dressed. She was shocked that He would ask her for anything.

Jesus then says something that is largely considered a figure of speech. Jesus said He would give her the "water of life." He wasn't speaking figuratively:

Then the angel showed me the river of the water of life, as clear as crystal, flowing from the throne of God and of the Lamb down the middle of the great street of the city. On each side of the river stood the tree of life, bearing twelve crops of fruit, yielding its fruit every month. And the leaves of the tree are for the healing of the nations.

Revelation 22:1-2

THE WOMAN'S SIN
4:16-26

Jesus asked the woman a question He already knew the answer to. Why did He start all this with a question? Why not just right away point out the woman's sin? Jesus used the Socratic method so often, it should make us wonder if Socrates himself was a plagiarizer.

Jesus knew that this was a loose woman and He wanted her to know that He knew, but that there was something much better in store for her today.

Jesus wanted her to experience the process of knowing Him. She got it that He knew the answer all along when she proclaimed that He was a prophet. Then she asked Him a strange question about where to worship, but we quickly see why.

Moses had promised that when the "Prophet" came, the one the Pharisees asked John about, that He would "explain all things." The woman wanted to know if the way the Samaritans worshipped was actually correct or not.

In a rare moment, Jesus plainly tells her no, that the Samaritans were wrong, but that in just a short while it wouldn't matter anymore. In an even more amazing moment of clarity not found in the gospels, Jesus clearly said that He was, in fact, the Messiah.

MY FOOD
4:27-38

Jesus' disciples were even more surprised to find Jesus talking to the woman than she was. It cannot be understated just how taboo this one-on-one conversation was.

The disciples had bought the food in town and now tried to get Jesus to eat, and He responded to them with a strange bit of obscurity. Why did Jesus say He had other food? He knew the disciples wouldn't get it. Why not speak to them as plainly as He just spoke to the woman?

John wants us to understand that Jesus has no desire to make our understanding of Him easy. As people, we like to figure things out. We like to solve puzzles. Jesus is not a puzzle to be solved. He is a man to be known. Jesus so rarely speaks clearly and straightforward that when He does later in John His disciples will shout for joy over it.

The parable about the harvester and reaper do not really seem to fit with what Jesus was explaining. To make things even more challenging for the disciples to understand, Jesus says that His food is actually His work. Work, especially the labor He speaks of here, actually makes us hungrier, not fed. How is it then that the Father's work fills us up?

SAMARITAN SALVATION
4:39-42

Before the disciples had much of a chance to think about this, the Samaritans find Jesus and beg Him to stay with them. Many believed because of the woman's testimony, but even more believed after they met Jesus. This must have been disorienting to the disciples and any Pharisee that heard about this. Jesus offered salvation and comfort to the Samaritans, but scorn for the Pharisees.

IN GALILEE
4:43-45

A couple days later when Jesus arrived in Galilee, He was well-received by the people who had seen or heard about His miracles in Jerusalem. They were looking forward to seeing more miracles there. Why did Jesus chastise them for wanting to see miracles?

John makes an interesting statement here that Jesus knew a prophet has no honor in His home. This is probably within parentheses in your Bible. Since there is no such punctuation in Greek this means the translators either saw this as added later or as an attempt at a parenthetical statement, or both. Often when you see parentheses in your Bible, one of these is the case.

Even though John does not say so, we know from the other gospels that Jesus was unable to do many miracles in Galilee because of the pervasive lack of faith in Him there. In fact, John tells us this bit of information here because we will only see one miracle, not many, before Jesus departs again for Jerusalem.

HEROD'S OFFICIAL
4:46-54

The fact that a "royal official," who is actually Herod's official, is the one person to be healed is again a slap in the face to the Jewish people and leadership. Herod was one of the most despised men in Israel. He claimed to be Israel's king from the lineage of David when he was barely a Jew himself, if one at all.

We see something powerful here, though. Herod's official worked for a wicked man, but he was a man full of faith. Like Daniel serving in Babylon, this man was willing to take Jesus at His word.

Because the man believed Jesus, his son was healed at the exact moment Jesus spoke it. This not only demonstrated the power of Jesus, but the power of faith in Him.

THE OUTCAST

John went out of his way in chapter four to point out that Jesus chose the outcasts to make His salvation and love known. Even speaking harshly to these outcasts, they still persisted for His favor. How often do we feel the Lord say "no" to us and give up? How often will we see the Pharisees reject Jesus for disagreeing with them or simply not getting their permission?

If we were to define faith simply from what we see here, it would look like not letting God tell us no. It would be that we do not try to change Him, but accept Him on His terms and still ask for Him to save us and heal us. We cannot change Him, but His heart is easily swayed by faith in Him.

Don't forget to read John this week!
READ IT | KNOW IT | LIVE IT
For the word of God is living and active. Sharper than any double-edged sword, it penetrates even to dividing soul and spirit, joints and marrow; it judges the thoughts and attitudes of the heart. (Hebrews 4:12)

JOHN 5-6

STUDY QUESTIONS

1. Why would Jesus ask the lame man if he *wants to* get well? Why is the man's response odd?

2. Why did Jesus ask the man to pick up his mat if He knew it was against the Jewish leaders' rule?

3. Why did the Jews want to kill Jesus for claiming to be equal with God?

4. Why doesn't Jesus just do what He wants? Why does He only do what He sees the Father doing?

5. Why does it matter who approves of Jesus' testimony?

6. Why won't Jesus accept glory from humans?

7. Why did Jesus test Phillip? Why would Andrew suggest using the boy's fish and loaves to feed so many?

8. Why did the people ask Jesus for a sign immediately after the miracle of food?

9. Why does Jesus make it intentionally hard for people to believe in Him by speaking about "eating His flesh?"

COMMENTARY NOTES

JOHN CHAPTER 5

Jesus' authority is one of the main themes in the book of John. It was the understanding of the Pharisees that they were the gatekeepers to become teachers in Israel. If you weren't taught by them, it was impossible to be approved by them. They granted authority to teach and lead the nation toward God.

THE POOL OF BETHESDA
5:1-4

This brings us to Jesus beginning to intentionally offend the Pharisees who already did not like Him since He hadn't sought their permission to teach.

Jesus went to the Pool of Bethesda and found an invalid waiting to get into the water. The thought was that there was an angel who would occasionally come down and stir up the waters, and the first person to get in after the angel had touched it would be healed. The sick would lie nearby and jump in quickly when it happened, or men like this invalid would use the kindness of a friend to throw him in.

We do not know whether this was superstition or if there were documented healings in the water, but we know that the lame were probably never the ones healed. This man had no one to help him in when the waters were randomly stirred up.

DO YOU WANT TO GET WELL?
5:5

Jesus asked this particular man a very pointed question to which he never answers. Jesus asked him if he wanted to get well, yet he never says yes. He gives an excuse as to why he isn't well. We will see a little more into this man's heart shortly.

Instead of dealing with this man's inability to answer a simple question, Jesus commands him to get up. John tells us that he immediately felt healed, so he picked up his mat and walked. If he hadn't felt healed first, would the man have had faith in Jesus' words?

How often do we make excuses before the Lord instead of asking Him for what we really want? How often do we ask for what we think God wants to hear instead of asking Him for what we truly need?

THE LAW PROHIBITS YOU
5:6-13

The man walked away with his mat and walked past a Jewish leader. When John says "Jewish leader," he is normally speaking of the Pharisees or Sadducees, the two groups of teachers that led Israel under the hospices of Roman rule.

The law that prohibited the man from carrying his mat was not a biblical command, but an official interpretation of that command the Pharisees had devised. Though John never specifically points this out, most of the points of disagreement between Jesus and the Pharisees that John will record have to do with their law, not God's.

When the leaders asked the man who had healed him, he honestly didn't know, but he could definitely tell that they wanted to hunt him down and discipline him for commanding the man to disobey their law.

STOP SINNING
5:14-15

Jesus sought out the man again and told him a very strange thing. Jesus tells the formerly crippled man to stop sinning or something worse than his former state would happen to him. What is worse than being an invalid for decades? We don't know, but Jesus assures him he doesn't want it.

Not all sickness is caused by sin, but sometimes it is, as clearly portrayed here. We must not make doctrinal or theological determinations from singular passages in scripture that we like or that fit our own narrative. That is what the Pharisees did. We must seek to know Jesus and walk in His wisdom in humility. That means sometimes wrestling with the fact that sin can cause us to be sick.

Jesus was very concerned about people repenting from their sin throughout the gospel. Unlike a modern version of the gospel that is proclaimed that says Jesus isn't concerned with people's sins, He knew it was our sins that lead our hearts away from Him. We do not wander away from God without cause, it is always our sin that leads us away.

This man showed that there was great bitterness in his heart. Even after he had been healed, he was angry enough at this response from Jesus that he went back to the Jewish leaders and ratted Jesus out. He knew the leaders were looking for something to accuse Jesus of, and he was willing to give it to them. How sad!

THE SON CAN DO NOTHING BY HIMSELF
5:16-21

This gave the Pharisees a case against Jesus and John tells us that they began to persecute Him. This wasn't a persecution of violence; not yet at least. It was a verbal assault against Him in public and in private, not doubt.

John gives us a synopsis of this persecution in verses 16-18 by giving Jesus' reply to them. He claimed that His Father was God Himself, something that angered the leaders to the point of wanting to outright kill Him.

Then John goes on to record a very detailed argument He gave to the Jewish leaders. It was Jesus' first answer to the accusation of His authority.

Jesus tells us some very important things in His response to the wicked leaders. He told them that the Father raises the dead to new life and that the Son (Him) had the power to grant that life too.

We must understand that half of the Jewish leadership, the Sadducees, did not believe in the resurrection of the dead. In fact, the Pharisees and Sadducees bitterly hated each other over this point.

THE FATHER JUDGES NO ONE
5:22-23

Jesus next introduces us to one of the most perplexing paradoxes in the book of John. It is one of the paradoxes we will revisit several times, one that John will not give us a clear answer to.

Jesus tells us that His Father judges no one, but that Jesus Himself, the Son, judges everyone. Jesus is going to say just the opposite very shortly, then flip it around yet again. The

35

paradox John gives us here is that neither the Father nor the Son judge, but at the same time they both do. This is a topic that John specifically calls our attention to that we must deal with.

Many people turn away from God today over the issue of judgment. People want to exist in their own self-righteousness, where they get to choose how bad is too bad for God's love. This is exactly what the Jewish leadership had done, and they had made sure those rules went in their favor.

In Revelation, our same author, John tells us that in the last days people will reject Jesus specifically because He has the right to judge. It is this issue of judgment that is one of the primary things John wants us to deal with in his gospel. If we accept Jesus as judge, we will accept His Father, but if we reject the Son's judgment, we also reject the Father.

We must choose to wrestle with the idea that we will one day be judged by God. No one wants to stand judgment, but we have no choice. How we deal with this reality will be a determining factor in our lives especially as the last days draw near.

ETERNAL LIFE
5:24-30

Jesus next tells us that if we hear His words and believe that the Father sent Him, we will have eternal life and be spared from judgment.

In verses 28-29 Jesus seems to quote the passage in Daniel where he is told that in the last days the hearts of men will be judged:

Multitudes who sleep in the dust of the earth will awake: some to everlasting life, others to shame and everlasting contempt.

Daniel 12:2

Once again, Jesus finishes this refrain with the reality of coming judgment. This time He says He only judges as the Father has instructed Him to.

TESTIMONY
5:31-38

In the Law, Moses tells us that the truth of a matter must be established by at least two or three witnesses.

One witness is not enough to convict anyone accused of any crime or offense they may have committed. A matter must be established by the testimony of two or three witnesses.

Deuteronomy 19:15

Jesus says that if He testifies about Himself, that His testimony is not true, based on this passage in Deuteronomy. Here again John will soon introduce a new paradox for us, but we will save that until we come to it. In this case, Jesus says that He does have another's testimony.

Jesus said that He does not accept human testimony, but for their sake, He references John the Baptist's testimony. He said that he was a lamp that gave them light and they were able to enjoy that light, but that Jesus' testimony was of much more value than John's.

What was Jesus testifying about? That He had seen God and had come from Him. Jesus is doing the very works He saw the Father do with His own eyes.

YOU SEARCH THE SCRIPTURES
5:39-47

Next Jesus makes a very pointed accusation against the Jewish leaders: that they do not even know God. He tells them that they search the scriptures because in them they will find the secret to eternal life, but that they have completely missed it because that secret was the very Man standing in front of them and they couldn't recognize Him.

Jesus said He didn't need them to honor Him, but if they truly loved God they would. Because they refused to honor Him, it proved that they did not truly have any love for God in their hearts.

John alludes to the reason as to why Jesus makes such a big deal about authority. Jesus obviously had been asked about where His authority came from and who testified in His favor. They would have expected that His mentor would honor and testify as to how He had studied under Him. Jesus tells them that they accept the honor and testimony of men, but when someone came from God with the testimony and authority of God Himself, they rejected it.

Jesus finishes His accusation against the Jewish leaders by telling them that even though He has the authority to accuse them before God of their sin, He doesn't need to. He tells them that Moses himself will accuse them, the one in whom they studied day and night, of their rejection of God.

Jesus is saying that the scriptures themselves, the ones they studied so diligently, spoke against their pride and arrogance. Surely Jesus had this scripture in the back of His mind when He said this:

> *For rebellion is like the sin of divination, and arro-*
> *gance like the evil of idolatry. Because you have re-*

jected the word of the LORD, he has rejected you as king

1 Samuel 15:23

This was the Lord's rejection of king Saul, and it is exactly the same thing Jesus is saying now to the current rulers of Israel. They have been rejected for their rebellion and arrogance.

JOHN CHAPTER 6

THE MIRACLE OF MULTIPLIED FOOD
6:1-15

Jesus has now gained a following of "multitudes." We are not told how many people, but we know that the healing of the royal official's son has impressed people. We also do not know if Jesus had performed more healings after that one, but it wouldn't be surprising once the crowds heard about it.

Jesus decided to cross the Sea of Galilee for reasons we are not told and the crowds followed Him. Think about that. They either had to load up in sail boats or walk across relatively rugged terrain (especially for we Westerners who drive everywhere). Jesus ends up stopping in the middle of nowhere and now the crowd that spontaneously followed Him is hungry.

The same God who had a spontaneous following that left Egypt will again feed His people with supernatural provision.

Jesus asked Philip a question John tells us He already knew the answer to. Here again we see Jesus asking questions just to test someone. Why does He do this, and does He still do it with us?

Philip's answer to where they could buy food for the crowd is honest and accurate. It would take a tremendous amount of money to buy a snack for everyone. Some view Philip's answer as a lack of faith, but that isn't what is happening here. Jesus wanted one of His disciples to express the truth of the situation through natural eyes. Sometimes our first course of action should be to address the problem head on instead of just feigning faith that God can do something.

Andrew then came up with the idea to share the little boy's food. We do not know what his motivation was behind this because John only lets us speculate. Was it faith for what Jesus was about to do? Was it that he thought there might be enough people with a little food in the crowd to share? Was he offering something so that only Jesus could eat, the one he thought would be his king?

5,000 MEN

Now we find out how many people had followed Jesus. 5,000 men does not mean 5,000 people. It means men. There were women and children for sure. This could easily have been between 10,000 and 20,000 people.

Jesus thanked His Father for the five loaves and two fish and then told His disciples to distribute them to the massive crowd. John doesn't tell us how the bread and fish multiplied. We don't know if they all saw it grow before their eyes or if it was more subtle than that. John forces our imaginations to wander here, but we do know that there was so much food that everyone was able to stuff themselves on free food and there was plenty left over.

Verse 14 seems to allude that it wasn't until this miracle was over did people realize what had happened. Maybe it was subtle, but the implication was clear; Jesus had to be the Prophet we keep hearing about.

MAKING JESUS KING

I don't know about you, but when I look at the leadership we constantly have to choose from in our nation, I'd just assume make a man who could multiply food and heal the sick ruler even if I had to do it by force. It only makes sense.

Jesus knew what was running through their hearts and He had to leave. Jesus was in fact King, but He could only accept His throne on His terms. Our same author, John, will later tell us in his book of Revelation how Jesus will return and take His throne as Ruler of eternity. This moment was not that, so Jesus escapes.

ON THE LAKE
6:16-24

John doesn't tell us if the disciples set out on the lake to look for Jesus or if they were going to a predetermined meeting point on the other side of the lake where they had started. Either way, what happened next is truly amazing.

If we saw Jesus walking on the water, I dare say we would be terrified at the sight as well. How many people have you seen walk on water? When we see things we do not understand and they go beyond understanding we are generally curious or afraid. Given the already difficult situation the disciples were in, it's not hard to understand why they were afraid when they saw Jesus on the water.

41

They were so afraid, in fact, that they refused to let Jesus in the boat until they heard His voice. Did John include this little tidbit for the sake of humor or to make a point that even though they recognized the activity of Jesus, they still needed to hear His voice? Either way, this story is still amazing almost 2,000 years later.

John offers another odd piece of information. The next day the crowd realized that Jesus and the disciples left separately, but that they did not return. Some large number of the crowd decided to board a boat and cross the lake to go looking for Jesus, although it would be hard to imagine that all 5,000 plus people boarded what boats had come.

IN THE SYNAGOGUE OF CAPERNAUM
6:25-70

Jesus doesn't seem to be very good at keeping a following. Today He would be a terrible leader in our eyes. In this passage, Jesus runs off all but twelve of His followers. That's a pretty terrible growth plan for someone bringing His kingdom down to earth—over 5,000 to twelve in a few short minutes!

The issue is that Jesus sees through the crowd's motivation. They came over looking for Jesus because He fed them. In those days, that meant more than just having cake in the break room at work. Food was hard to come by back then. Jesus had the first and only fast-food establishment in the world, and they wanted more.

The crowd that crossed the lake had found Him inside the Synagogue of Capernaum, likely where they saw a crowd. Jesus was teaching and they interrupted with their questions.

Someone in the crowd recognized the similarity between Jesus feeding them fish and bread in a deserted place and God giving them quail and manna in the desert centuries before. He asked Jesus what sign He could show that proved He was from God to back up the miracle He had performed.

This is where we need to understand the meaning of the word "sign." Many misunderstand this to be the people asking for another miracle, but that isn't what they are asking for.

> *If a prophet, or one who foretells by dreams, appears among you and announces to you a sign or wonder, and if the sign or wonder spoken of takes place, and the prophet says, "Let us follow other gods" (gods you have not known) "and let us worship them," you must not listen to the words of that prophet or dreamer. The Lord your God is testing you to find out whether you love him with all your heart and with all your soul.*

> *Deuteronomy 13:1-3*

Here we see that the Lord allowed signs to accompany prophets, even those who weren't necessarily from Him. A sign, in this usage, is something that man cannot control. When Moses parted the Red Sea, that was something beyond the control of Moses to do of his own accord. The same with the Jordan river. The sign Joshua had was that the sun stayed in the sky longer than normal to complete a battle (Joshua 10:12-13).

These are the kinds of things that no human can control, and when these signs happen as they foretell, it attests to their message being genuinely divine. In that way, the people are asking for Jesus to show them another sign that He was to predict before it happened. Because Jesus had blessed the food before it multiplied, it would have been a miracle to them, not a sign.

Jesus then tells them that it wasn't Moses giving the people manna and that it wasn't bread that Jesus had multiplied by some trick, but by the same power as the manna. Jesus Himself was this power. He was this bread of life.

This they could not accept. They knew Jesus in Capernaum. They knew His "father," or so they thought. How could He be the bread that came down from heaven? Then Jesus went a step too far and told them that unless they ate of His flesh, His "bread," that they could not have eternal life.

This is such a normal religious term that Christians have used throughout the centuries, we often fail to understand its significance. We understand that Jesus was speaking figuratively, but it sounded to them just like what Jesus was proposing: cannibalism.

Jesus then told them that if they ate His flesh, they would never die like their ancestors had. It was just too much. In just a short while, Jesus ran off all of His followers by saying things too offensive for them to accept.

Jesus then tells His remaining disciples something powerful—that they the Father had actually drawn them close to Him to believe. But even in those that remained, one of them would betray Jesus and He knew it and declared it right then.

How odd that day must have been for the disciples. They must have felt a little sorry for Jesus, a little proud to be the ones who stuck around and a little confused by everything He had said. Jesus had gone from being the nice guy who fed everyone to being the one who offended thousands with a few simple words. What a day.

JOHN 7-8

STUDY QUESTIONS

1. What does Jesus mean by saying that His "time is not yet here?"

2. Why is Jesus' teaching not His own?

3. Why do they say that no one will know where the Messiah comes from and then say that they know the Messiah will come from Bethlehem?

4. Why doesn't Jesus tell the Jews He is from Bethlehem?

5. Why doesn't Jesus condemn the woman? What does Jesus mean that He came to fulfill the law and not to destroy it?

6. Why does Jesus say He has much to say in judgment of the Jews, but earlier He has said He does not judge them?

7. Why would the Jews accuse Jesus of being demon possessed and a Samaritan? Why was being a Samaritan a bad thing?

COMMENTARY NOTES

JOHN CHAPTER 7

ACTING IN SECRET
7:1-13

This chapter starts with an interesting "after this." It seems like this was a watershed moment in Jesus' ministry. After everyone left Him, Jesus needed to decide what to do next. It was obvious that He had quite the following before His offensive words, but now what was He to do?

Jesus chose not to travel to Judea where "His disciples could see His works," as His brother so eloquently put it, but to stay in Galilee for a while. The Jewish leaders wanted Him dead, and as John has already told us, Jesus did not need any man's praise or testimony.

This is an example of some of the mystery of Jesus that has befuddled mankind as long as we have read the New Testament. Why was Jesus so intent on staying hidden?

In the Gospels we see Jesus repeatedly hiding away, telling others not to talk about Him and trying to perform miracles in secret. It all seemed to be tied to "His time" as it is here. Jesus tells His brothers that it is not His time yet, but for them any time will do.

The fact that John points out that Jesus' brothers do not yet believe in Him points to the tone of their comment. It sounds like Jesus' brothers telling Him to go to the Feast of Tabernacles to gain a large following again is tongue in cheek. They are mocking Him for having a following and losing it.

Jesus' response to them is very interesting. Jesus said He was not going to the festival, but then He later goes in secret. Why did Jesus seemingly lie to His brothers?

The issue here is in the Greek behind this statement. The connotation, and even in some manuscripts specifically, the meaning here is that Jesus is saying He is not going with them, or not yet. His family would have gone to the festival before it began and stayed the entire time. Jesus wasn't going with them, but He didn't intend for them to understand He wasn't going.

Jesus gave the Jewish leaders just enough time to give up looking for Him before He showed Himself publicly. He was there the whole time, but He never exposed Himself where anyone could see Him.

Everyone at the festival knew that the leaders were looking for Jesus to either question or arrest Him. This got everyone talking about Jesus, and surely John and the disciples overheard a lot of it. Jesus probably heard His fair share of conversations about Him as He clandestinely moved through the crowds.

Tabernacles was a time when people were supposed to build a temporary shelter for themselves out in the streets or in courtyards for a week to remember that they lived in temporary dwellings for forty years after they left Egypt. It must have been thick with booths and people and merchants and kids running wild.

It's not terribly hard to see how Jesus could have hidden Himself or that He and the others would have been privy to everyone whispering about Jesus with one eye open for Pharisees and Sadducees.

It must have been somewhat fun for Jesus to hear people talking about whether He was or wasn't a good man. Think of all the justifications people gave for and against. Think about how embarrassing it must have been for a few people to recognize the man in the robe teaching at the temple as the same man in the same robe hanging out near their booth in town.

JESUS TEACHES IN THE TEMPLE
7:14-24

In the temple, John does not tell us what Jesus taught but only the conversation that takes place afterward. The thing that amazed everyone was that Jesus knew and understood the scriptures and how to interpret them without having been taught. They knew this because the Jewish teaching was entirely an oral tradition.

At this point in history, Jews would read and have read to them the Old Testament, but they also had a completely oral tradition on the official interpretations and backstories behind the scriptures. They dared not write them down for fear that people would take them as seriously as the scriptures themselves, and so they would know who had and had not studied, because it would have only been people they orally taught.

Jesus was not among that group.

If you ever had a chance to read the Talmud, the now written version of the ancient oral tradition, you know it is very insightful. Remember that it is not scripture itself, and should not be thought of in such a high regard, but much of it is very informative into how Jews think and thought then. It has stories that the New Testament references as true, but also many stories that are obviously tall tales and some teaching that is abhorrent. In the gospels, Jesus even attests to the truth of some of the Talmud while condemning parts of it.

Yet here is Jesus, who had not studied the Talmud from the leaders, reciting proper understanding of the scripture itself. This is why they were amazed, because none of the leaders had taught Jesus and they all knew it.

Jesus tells them that He gained His learning from Someone other than Himself, just as they did, but that His learning came directly from God. He then accuses them of breaking the law of Moses for plotting to kill Him. It is this point that no one knew publicly yet, but it had already been discussed by the leaders.

To this, the crowd of non-Jewish leaders told Him that He must be demon-possessed because they hadn't heard such a thing. It is important to realize here that the Jewish leaders were silent on this matter, because they already knew what they were planning. It was the crowds who were ignorant, and the leaders let them speak up.

Jesus wasn't actually speaking to the crowds, but to the small minority of leaders there that day. He was speaking directly to them, in fact, when He told them that they wanted to kill Him for healing someone on the Sabbath.

If you read the Old Testament and think it is long, then you're right, but it wasn't long enough for the Pharisees. After the Babylonian captivity, they wanted to make sure that Israel never neglected the commands of God again, so they began to elaborate on what each command of God meant. That quickly turned into laws on top of laws on top of laws.

For most of the 613 commandments of the Old Testament, there may be several instructions for each in the Talmud. The Jewish leadership had a list of things it was lawful to do on the Sabbath, like circumcising a child, that are not pre-scribed in scripture. Because healing a blind man is not specifically mentioned in the Talmud, they were angry at Jesus, who they thought should have known better.

In the end, the Talmudic commandments often worked to the betterment of those in power over those without authority and they largely dealt with outward appearances. Jesus thrusts this problem front and center here.

SURELY THIS MAN IS THE PROPHET
7:25-53

Now we see that word of the Jewish leaders plot to kill Je-sus has leaked a little bit across Jerusalem. Because a few knew this and they hadn't arrested Him, people began to assume that the leaders had come to approve of Jesus. This talk must have been odious to the Jewish leaders.

Their last statement brings us back to one of the primary paradoxes of the book of John, Jesus' origins. Here the people say that they know where Jesus is from, but they won't know where the Messiah is from. This is a point that goes back and forth throughout the book because it was either important for them to know where the Messiah was from or that he was unknown depending on the situation. It is obvious they use this notion as a way to discredit Jesus as it suited them.

Jesus told them that He spoke on the authority of someone else, and from their response, they knew He meant God the Father. He angered the crowd enough to move them to violence by telling them they didn't know God, something we will see several times in John. Jesus did not mince words when it came to people's deception and sin, but He rarely spoke clearly about His own deity.

It was when people starting talking seriously about Jesus as the Messiah that drove the Pharisees to give arrest orders for Jesus, but again thwarts any attempts to capture Him.

Before leaving, Jesus proclaimed one more time, as He did to the Samaritan woman at the well, that He was the water of life. John now tells us that Jesus is speaking specifically about the Holy Spirit who was to come when Jesus had been resurrected and ascended to heaven in His glory.

John again points out that the crowd is interested in knowing whether Jesus is the Prophet or the Messiah and it leads them back to the paradox of Jesus' origins. Those who opposed Jesus as the Messiah claimed that He couldn't be the Messiah since He wasn't from David's line or from Bethlehem.

Why doesn't Jesus take the time to correct them? Wouldn't it have been so much easier if Jesus had just plainly told them that He was from Bethlehem? That He was the one who Anna and Simeon had prophesied about when they met Him in the temple as a baby? That He was the one Herod had tried to kill and the Magi had visited? Why didn't Jesus tell them He was the one the shepherds of Bethlehem came to visit?

Even Nicodemus tried to stick up for Jesus among the Sanhedrin, but they quickly shot him down on this point. They thought Jesus was from Galilee where He had been raised. There are no Old Testament scriptures about any prophet or the Messiah coming from Galilee, so even Nicodemus had no reply. He had come to believe Jesus was the Messiah, but he couldn't answer this question because of a simple misunderstanding Jesus allowed to persist.

JOHN CHAPTER 8

THE WOMAN CAUGHT IN ADULTERY
8:1-11

Most Bibles point out that the earliest known manuscripts of John do not include this story. It is included in our modern Bibles because it has been recognized by most Christians throughout history to be authentic. It may have been one that John and the other apostles told so often that it was later appended, or maybe it was one that some had maliciously cut out for some reason and later appropriately added back in. Whatever the case, no translator will remove it because it has been one of the greatest stories of Jesus' grace and mercy in the Gospels.

The teachers of the law really wanted to way to catch Jesus openly ignorant of or breaking the law. This story is the best of their failed attempts at it.

The point of bringing the woman to Jesus was to trap Him by having Jesus condemn her alone, as opposed to she and the man she was caught with.

If a man commits adultery with another man's wife—with the wife of his neighbor—both the adulterer and the adulteress are to be put to death.

Leviticus 20:10

Jesus refused to condemn her, though. What Jesus does next, however, has befuddled people for ages. Instead of immediately responding, Jesus bent down and began doodling in the sand. John does not tell us what He wrote.

Why would John mention that Jesus wrote in the sand, but not tell us what He wrote? This is so strange, but John must have certainly done it for a reason. He is being intentionally subtle, when at other times John is very descriptive, so we must reason this is on purpose.

The men accusing the woman began to leave one at a time, not because Jesus told the ones without sin to cast the first stone, but because of what He continued to write in the sand.

The reason John's silence on what Jesus wrote is so significant is because John tells us that they all left one by one, beginning with the oldest. Was Jesus writing something specific about each one? Was He pointing out sins? We simply do not know what Jesus wrote, but we know it was powerful, and with this knowledge John leaves us in question.

Here again lies the genius of our author. John is more interested in us knowing Jesus than knowing about Him. Jesus wasn't giving us a tool to use in our lives against accusers, but was responding to the Spirit in that moment.

The last thing Jesus tells the woman is for her to leave her life of sin. We must not read this passage and assume Jesus did not care about the sin. He cared deeply. He knew better than the men accusing the woman how deeply her sin had destroyed her and how it would continue to do so. Jesus not condemning the woman is not Him condoning her sin, but Him releasing her from it. That is why we must consider Jesus' actions and His words very carefully in this passage.

JUDGMENT
8:12-30

Jesus moves on with an interesting statement. Jesus proclaims that He is the light of the world. This may seem to be a fun figure of speech, but He is in fact being eternally literal. We find out in Revelation that Jesus and the Father will be the only light in eternity—there will be no more sun or stars. The only lights of eternity come from Them (Revelation 22:5).

John tells us that the Pharisees question Jesus again about His testimony. This goes back to the recurring theme of who taught Jesus. In their oral teaching tradition, the teacher could vouch for the student and once the student had sufficiently passed their tests, the teacher would testify on their behalf. Jesus had no such teacher or testimony.

Jesus tells them that even if He did testify on His own behalf, it would still be true because He had come from heaven. Jesus then speaks to the greatest paradox in the book of John.

Jesus tells the people that He judges no one, but He has already said the contrary and He will say to the contrary again. Why does Jesus make His language about judgment so obscure? Why does Jesus in one breath say He judges and in another that He does not?

Jesus immediately casts judgment upon those listening by telling them that they will die in their sins, and they will not join Him. They obviously do not understand what He means, but Jesus quickly continues by telling them that He has much to say in judgment of them. Again, why does Jesus seem to flip-flop on this?

John never gives us a clear answer to this as the book goes on. All we know is that either He or the Father will certainly judge us, but exactly how that will work, we do not know.

This is an important point for us to consider. More and more people today use John as a proof-text for Jesus not judging anyone, but only loving and accepting them. They hand-pick the passages they like, where Jesus says He doesn't judge, and ignore the passages where He says He does. We must consider the fact again that John is not allowing us to pick and choose the Jesus we want, but he introduces intentional paradoxes so that we must confront any and all wayward thoughts we have about God and Jesus.

This paradox of judgment is one of the principle difficulties John makes us face. If we choose to believe one or the other, we choose to believe in a Jesus of our hand-picking. A Jesus of our making. We must choose to believe in the Jesus as John reveals Him, one that is too complex to understand without knowing Him personally.

I AM
8:31-58

Jesus now doubles down on His offensive language toward the Pharisees and Jewish leaders. He tells them they are slaves to sin, that they are children of the devil (not of Abraham as they thought) and that they have no relationship to God the Father.

All this definitely makes the leaders angry, but Jesus saves the most offensive thing He has said yet for last. Jesus told the Pharisees that Abraham rejoiced to see the day they were living in because He, the Messiah, would have come into the world. Jesus then said that Abraham saw it and was glad.

The Pharisees were thinking that it would have been impossible for Abraham to see Jesus because He was less than fifty years old. They were thinking literally, but so was Jesus. Jesus wasn't less than fifty years old. In fact, they were speaking to the One who is ageless. They were speaking to the very one who had no creator or beginning. They were speaking to the One who existed inside, outside and around time itself.

The final straw for these wicked men was when Jesus said that He was "I Am." This was the very name God had used of Himself when Moses asked who he should tell the Israelites had sent him (Exodus 3:13-15). This is one of the most holy names of God, and the fact that Jesus had claimed it of Himself sent the Pharisees in to a rage.

They immediately bent down to pick up stones to kill Him. Imagine yourself being so arrogant that you would immediately choose to put someone to death for something they said. This was an immediate group reaction. Jesus was showing them the violence they carried in their hearts.

John doesn't tell these stories in the same stroke of the pen on accident. This chapter began with these same leaders wanting to stone a woman and now they want to stone Jesus. These men's violence, anger, rage, hypocrisy, jealousy and bitterness were on full display, but they could not see it.

Don't forget to read John this week!
READ IT | KNOW IT | LIVE IT

For the word of God is living and active. Sharper than any double-edged sword, it penetrates even to dividing soul and spirit, joints and marrow; it judges the thoughts and attitudes of the heart. (Hebrews 4:12)

JOHN 9-10

STUDY QUESTIONS

1. Why did the disciples ask if the blind man sinned or his parents? Did Jesus rebuke them for this thinking?

2. Why did Jesus spit in the mud to heal the man? Was this necessary?

3. Why did God allow this man to live with blindness for so long only to be a sign to others of God's glory?

4. Why would the Pharisees be better off if they were actually blind? Why does their guilt remain by being able to see?

5. Why does Jesus liken Himself to a shepherd? How can we hear Jesus' voice?

6. Why does Jesus tell the leaders that scripture had called us "gods?" Why won't Jesus answer their question as to whether or not He is the Messiah?

COMMENTARY NOTES

JOHN CHAPTER 9

THE MAN BORN BLIND HEALED
9:1-7

This chapter begins with an awkward question. There was a commonly held belief that all sickness was attributable to some kind of sin, either personal sin or generational. As they stood near this man, the disciples pondered aloud this doctrine.

It is important to note that in His response, Jesus never tells the disciples that sin is not a cause of sickness. In fact, we have already seen that Jesus alludes to that very fact when He healed the paralytic earlier in the book. But here Jesus introduces something completely new.

Jesus tells them that this man was born blind so that in this very moment in time he could be healed and thereby display the glory of God. This brings us to a very difficult and painful question: did God make this man blind so that he could suffer without sight for years just for this moment? Does He do the same kind of thing today?

If this is true, it may really cause us to wrestle with the very nature of God and how we think of Him. Does the Lord allow us to suffer, and if so, why? This is again a place where John forces us to come to know Jesus Himself as opposed to only knowing about Him. If we only know about Him, we will be horribly offended by passages like this. If we know Him personally, we have a place to go for the an-

swers we need. This is one of those places where our answers can only be found in our relationship with Jesus.

The way Jesus chose to heal this young man is interesting.
He spit in the dirt and made mud and wiped it on the eyes
of the man, then told him to wash the mud off. We have
already seen Jesus merely speak healing over a boy who
was in another town. Why did Jesus need to perform an
action?

We will shortly see that Jesus intentionally chose to perform the simplest and silliest of actions to have this man
receive his healing to rouse the ire of the Pharisees. This
miracle was performed on the Sabbath, so this ridiculous
act was to prove a point to the Jewish leadership about
themselves, a point that again goes right over their heads.

AN IMPROMPTU TRIAL
9:8-19

The man went and washed in the pool of Siloam just as
Jesus had instructed, and immediately he could see. It is
important to note that He did not see until this happened,
so until now he has only heard Jesus' voice, but not seen
him.

This gets everyone in Jerusalem talking now because they
all knew that this young man had been born blind. They
had encountered him in the markets and around Jerusalem
begging. Now that he was healed, they wanted to know
how it happened.

The way the man was healed rapidly throws the entire city
into trouble. It was an obvious miracle that a man born
blind could see, but the way it happened seemed to break

the law. How could it not be God who healed him, but how could God break His own law, or so they thought?

This caught the attention of the Pharisees who began questioning him to get to the bottom of things. They argued amongst themselves about these questions. Who other than God could heal this man, but how could God ask the man to "work" on the Sabbath?

The way this passage ends is with a specific kind of skepticism that the Pharisees held. They did not believe that the man had been born blind. How could that be, considering there were already multiple testimonies saying he had? Remember that they believed a matter had to be established on the witness of two or three witnesses?

The Pharisees were selectively skeptical of miracles that didn't fit within their hypocritical boxes. On the positive side, they wanted to know for sure that a miracle was from God, and not an elaborate plan to fool people. It may seem implausible, but it is theoretically possible for two parents to concoct a plan to teach their son how to act blind so that some day a decade or two in the future they could proclaim him healed and somehow make money off of it.

This was the thing the Pharisees wanted to sort out. It was inconceivable to them that a true man of God could ask this man to do something as simple as washing his eyes on the Sabbath, even if that meant being healed after a lifetime of blindness.

The Pharisees called in the man's parents and questioned them, but they shrunk under the pressure of the moment. John now shows us that the Pharisees had their suspicions of just who was behind this, even though the blind man hadn't named him. They knew it was Jesus, and the parents already knew that the Pharisees were prejudiced against Him, so they refused to answer for fear of losing their place in Jewish society.

We see now the depth of the Pharisees prejudice and hypocrisy when they bait the man again by telling him that they knew the man who healed him is a sinner. To this, the man gives one of the most famous and well-reasoned responses in the Bible:

"One thing I do know. I was blind but now I see!"

The conversation with the man deteriorated from this point on because he refused to say what the Pharisees wanted to hear. They argued back and forth for a while, but the straw that broke the camel's back was when the formerly blind man told them that he was incredulous at their ignorance of where this man had come from.

Remember how often this has now come up? The Pharisees keep changing their mind about whether they will know or not know where the Messiah comes from. This time they say that since they do not know where Jesus came from, He cannot be the Messiah because the argument works in their favor here. When the man chastised them for not knowing, they insulted him.

Their insult is indicative of how deeply entrenched in their own wrong theology they were. The chapter started out with the question of whose sin had caused his blindness, and now the Pharisees confirm what the young man had probably heard for most of his life; that he was a wretched sinner from the day of his birth, separated from God for something he never understood.

TRUE BLINDNESS
9:35-41

It seems rather funny that Jesus let the man handle himself before the Pharisees alone, but he did pretty well. Even though Jesus' name had never come up between the man and the Pharisees, it was obvious the young man and everyone else knew who had healed him.

Jesus found him and asked if he now believed in the "Son of Man." This is such an odd title for Jesus, but He uses it often. John is trying diligently to show that Jesus is the Son of God, part of the Godhead Himself, but he continually references when Jesus calls Himself the Son of Man. Why?

This brings us to the paradox of Jesus being fully man and fully God. How can He be both at the same time? In what ways did Jesus lay down His deity and take on flesh and in what ways did human nature not affect or overcome Him? This duality of nature has racked the minds of the brightest men and women throughout history and it still lingers with us today. It is another paradox that can only be solved by knowing Jesus as opposed to knowing about Him.

Jesus again doubles down on the paradox of judgment. He tells the Pharisees, who were there listening and observing Jesus allowing this man to worship Him, that it was specifically for judgment that He came to the world.

How does Jesus play this judgment thing so many ways? Which is it; did Jesus come to judge or not?

This passage illustrates the duality of this judgment very well. By asking Jesus if they were blind too, Jesus gives them some of the worst news in John.

Because they thought they saw clearly, Jesus told them the guilt of their sin and hypocrisy remained. It is like Jesus' was saying to them, "You only wish that you were so lucky as to be blind!"

This man may have suffered his entire life up to this point with blindness, but the principle takeaway here is that his blindness eventually led to eternal sight. God truly cares about us and the suffering we experience in this life, but what He cares about immeasurably more is our eternal fate.

We know that because the Pharisees thought they saw clearly but were dead wrong about Jesus, that their guilt remained. Had they been blissfully ignorant of Jesus, perhaps there would have been mercy. For this man, he became an experience that God used the same as the prophet Hosea.

God asked Hosea to suffer the emotional scars of marrying an adulterous woman so that he could understand the emotional pain God experienced at the hands of adulterous Israel. He asked this young man to live blind for part of his short life so that he would know true sight for eternity. There is no one better who understood in the book of John that Jesus was his path toward eternal sight.

When it came to Jesus' judgment, the one who everyone saw as blind would be guiltless and the ones who thought they saw would be judged guilty. How backwards and upside down!

JOHN CHAPTER 10

SHEEP METAPHORS
10:1-21

Many people today think that Jesus used sheep metaphors because everyone understood what He would have meant back then, but we see here that's just not true. Even though people were more accustomed to being around sheep back then, Jesus was using a figure of speech He knew the Pharisees wouldn't understand. To make matters worse, Jesus even addressed this metaphor directly at them.

Unfortunately, a common misunderstanding about Jesus' parables and figures of speech is that He spoke them so that most people would understand, but in fact it was for just the opposite reason. Jesus spoke in parables and figures of speech in such a way that no one could understand. He was intentionally obscure.

Jesus did this so that no one would understand Him. He wasn't interested in people figuring Him out, He wanted people to know Him. Jesus was using the parables and metaphors to find people intrigued enough to come to Him later and ask Him questions. Jesus knew that hungry hearts would seek Him out and try to learn what He meant, while those who were arrogant or disinterested would just move on.

In the case of the shepherd and the sheep, Jesus gives it to the Pharisees three different ways. He tells them that only the true shepherd is allowed through the gate—in this case the gate is God's approval. Jesus tells the Pharisees that sheep will follow the true shepherd because they know His voice. He's taking a direct shot at their illegitimacy because they do not love or know God because they do not know His voice.

Next, Jesus tells them that He is the gate in His parable. He is the one who has authority to allow in true teachers or to deny them. Again, Jesus is addressing this directly to the illegitimacy of the Pharisees because they have not known Him.

Lastly, Jesus calls Himself the good shepherd. He calls Himself the good shepherd specifically because He will lay down His life for His sheep. Jesus contrasts His love and devotion to His people with the Pharisees "looking out for number one" mentality. They were more interested in themselves; their honor, their money and their dignity than they were those they taught.

Because Jesus spoke to them so obscurely, many thought He was crazy, but for others the miracles Jesus had performed caused them to think twice about dismissing Him, even if they didn't understand what He was saying.

JESUS AT HANUKKAH
10:22-42

John tells us that Hanukkah fell during winter this particular year. This may seem strange, but because Hanukkah can move in the year because of its relationship to the lunar calendar, it can happen in the fall or the winter. Generally it falls around Christmastime, but it can happen as early as Thanksgiving (US holidays).

It was at this time that the Jewish leadership asked Jesus point blank whether or not He was the Messiah.

Again, Jesus does not answer them as clearly as they asked, but pointed to the works He had been doing and the fact that He had been doing them in the name of the Father God.

It was because Jesus claimed the ability to offer eternal life that those there picked up stones to stone Him. This was tantamount to claiming to be God Himself, the only one who could offer eternal life.

When Jesus saw the people pick up stones to execute Him, He pointed again to the miracles He had performed and asked them why they wanted to kill Him.

When they said that He was claiming to be God, blasphemy in their mind, Jesus turned their own words against them. Jesus quoted Psalm 82 to show them that even the Father had called His chosen people "gods."

This is interesting that they refuse to listen or accept this, since they have already argued with Jesus that they themselves are God's sons—that they were not illegitimate. But at this point, the Jewish leaders have no interest in listening to Jesus try and reason with them, so Jesus escapes from them unharmed. He went across the Jordan river to where John the Baptist had been to get away from Jerusalem.

Our author points out that the people there realized that John the Baptist had prophesied accurately about Jesus, but that he had never performed a "sign."

What they meant was that John never had a sign that attested to his authority before God. Again, a "sign" to the Jews is something that would accompany the works of a prophet so God could authenticate his message. It was something that the prophet could announce in advance that was outside the control of man. A sign would be like the Red Sea parting before Moses or the Jordan before Joshua. It was God's way of saying, I approve of this message.

John never showed a sign, but he was commonly held to be a prophet. That is probably because John prophesied so often to individual people about their lives the way he did with Herod, which led to his untimely death.

It was because of John's testimony of Jesus, however, that led many of the people who had encountered John years earlier to put their faith in Jesus now.

Don't forget to read John this week!
READ IT | KNOW IT | LIVE IT
For the word of God is living and active. Sharper than any double-edged sword, it penetrates even to dividing soul and spirit, joints and marrow; it judges the thoughts and attitudes of the heart. (Hebrews 4:12)

JOHN 11-12

STUDY QUESTIONS

1. Why was Jesus so obscure about Lazarus being dead?

2. Why was Jesus so emotional at Lazarus' tomb? Who was He weeping over?

3. Why does God use Caiaphas to prophesy about Jesus' death? Why would the Jewish leaders think they should or could kill Lazarus?

4. How did John know Judas helped himself to what was in the money bag?

   Why did Jesus allow this?

   Why did Jesus choose Judas in the first place if He would have known this about him?

5. Why did God prophesy in advance about people not believing in Jesus' message? Why would God want people's eyes blinded?

COMMENTARY NOTES

JOHN CHAPTER 11

LAZARUS
11:1-37

When confronted with the fact of Lazarus' sickness and impending death, Jesus tells the disciples it's time to go visit him. They object because Bethany is practically Jerusalem and they are afraid for Jesus' life.

Jesus tells them that He is the light of the world again and that as long as He is around, people can see, but when He is gone, people will stumble for darkness. Then Jesus continues on in speaking obscurely to them by talking about how Lazarus has "fallen asleep" meaning that he had died.

Why does Jesus so often speak obscurely, even to His disciples? They do not seem to be too intimidated to ask Jesus the point blank questions that get them answers, while everyone else is too afraid or arrogant to ask Him questions. Even when the disciples are slow to understand or a little dull in their perception, they are constantly engaged in conversation with Jesus. That is why they get straight answers.

That is when Jesus tells them that Lazarus is dead and that His plan all along was to go and work a miracle that would build their faith. That is why Jesus waited an extra two days after He learned of Lazarus' sickness. He wanted him to die. Again, just like the man born blind, this is a very challenging idea to wrestle with, that Jesus would have wanted things this way. It is something John tells us without apology, something he wants us to consider as we choose to know Jesus.

Thomas' statement about dying "with him," could mean either Lazarus or Jesus. It could have been that he meant that the disciples should go back to Judea, where Jesus was a wanted man, and die with Him.

When Jesus arrived back in Bethany, a walk of several days from across the Jordan, they find that Lazarus is in fact dead. When Mary and Martha sent for Jesus, it was probably a two day walk to tell Him, then He waited two more days and then walked back to Bethany in two days. In all, at least six days had passed since the message had gone out and now Lazarus had been in his tomb for four days. It may have been that Lazarus was dead before the sister's messenger had even reached Jesus and the disciples.

Everyone believes that Jesus could have healed Lazarus because He was the Man who had opened the eyes of the blind man, possibly Jesus' most famous miracle up to this point. Mary and Martha both tell Jesus that they are sure he wouldn't have died if Jesus had come sooner. They believe a little, but their faith is still weak. Even Martha knows that Jesus will raise Lazarus up in the resurrection, an astonishing statement, but she cannot fathom what is about to happen.

When Jesus was led to the tomb where Lazarus was, He erupted into the shortest verse in the Bible.

At the original writing, however, there were no chapter or verses. It was over a thousand years before they would appear to make referencing things easier for us today. It is probably because of the difficulty in understanding why Jesus wept that this is the shortest verse in the Bible. Those who assembled scriptures into verses probably set it apart because no one truly understands why He wept.

Was it because He was sad over Lazarus' death? Was He mourning? Was it because He was overcome by the emotions of Mary, Martha and those with them? We may never know for sure until we meet Jesus face to face, but it is no accident that John doesn't tell us. Although the disciples asked Jesus about almost everything, it may be that neither John nor the other disciples asked Jesus why He wept, so they don't know either.

What is important for us to know is that the God who created us and came to redeem us with His own blood has great emotions. It may be foreign to think of God as having emotions, but He is moved deeply by them. Becoming more familiar with the whole of scripture, it will become clear that God has passion for His people. He deeply loves, He deeply cares and He is mostly happy with us. Unfortunately, that is not how most people see God.

Although we do not know why, John wanted us to experience the depth with which the Son of God, the God-Man Himself, experienced emotion.

LAZARUS RAISED
11:38-44

In those days, most people could not afford embalming like we do today to most corpses. In fact, tombs were only a temporary holding place for corpses while they decomposed. After there was nothing left of a body but bones, they would be transferred out of the tomb and into an ossuary (bone box) and placed in a family plot.

Martha points out that if Jesus rolls away the stone and goes in to retrieve Lazarus, it will smell putrid. Martha didn't understand that Jesus intended for Lazarus to walk out under his own power.

It is a beautiful statement He makes to Martha here. We do not know when He said it, but sometime in the past Jesus promised Martha that if she only believed in Him she would see the power of God. How amazing to be able to say that you saw the power of God displayed by the very creator Himself, in the flesh!

Jesus then prays the most powerful "sermon-in-a-prayer" ever prayed. He points out to those there that God always hears His Son and will answer Him. Jesus is pointing out that it is not He who raises Lazarus, but the power of God the Father, in response to the prayer of the Son, who raises him. This is important because John has made a point to list all the times when Jesus says He does nothing of His own accord, but only in conjunction with the will of the Father.

Jesus speaks with that authority, not from Himself, but from His Father, when He commands Lazarus to come out.

One final thing to think of before we move on: was it necessary for Jesus to command only Lazarus to come out to prevent all the dead bodies inside from raising from the dead?

KILLING JESUS
11:45-57

Whether it was to try and sway the affections of the Sanhedrin or simply to report to them so they could lay a plot, we do not know, but someone went to them to let them know what Jesus had done. Swiftly, they gathered together to find out what to do about Jesus.

How sad a day that must have been! Upon hearing the news that Jesus had literally raised a man from the dead who had been in the tomb four days they had no inclination to ask whether He was truly from God or not. At this point, nothing could change their minds—not even a man literally coming back from the dead.

It was for this reason that Jesus, as recorded in Luke 16, told the story of Lazarus and the rich man:

> "There was a rich man who was dressed in purple and fine linen and lived in luxury every day. At his gate was laid a beggar named Lazarus, covered with sores and longing to eat what fell from the rich man's table. Even the dogs came and licked his sores.

> "The time came when the beggar died and the angels carried him to Abraham's side. The rich man also died and was buried. In Hades, where he was in torment, he looked up and saw Abraham far away, with Lazarus by his side. So he called to him, 'Father Abraham, have pity on me and send Lazarus to dip the tip of his finger in water and cool my tongue, because I am in agony in this fire.'

> "But Abraham replied, 'Son, remember that in your lifetime you received your good things, while Lazarus received bad things, but now he is comforted here and you are in agony. And besides all this, between us and you a great chasm has been set in place, so that those who want to go from here to you cannot, nor can anyone cross over from there to us.'

> "He answered, 'Then I beg you, father, send Lazarus to my family, for I have five brothers. Let him warn them, so that they will not also come to this place of torment.'

"Abraham replied, 'They have Moses and the Prophets; let them listen to them.'

"'No, father Abraham,' he said, 'but if someone from the dead goes to them, they will repent.'

"He said to him, 'If they do not listen to Moses and the Prophets, they will not be convinced even if someone rises from the dead.'"

Luke 16:19-31

The point here is that if people do not believe the testimony of scripture, even a man who came back from the dead will not sway them. How true this parable was of the Jewish leadership. It was no accident that the subject of this parable's name was Lazarus.

In their deliberations the high priest Caiaphas spoke up. God can always use willing vessels, but sometimes He will use the most hard-hearted and wicked vessels to carry out His will and speak His Word. Unknowingly, Caiaphas prophesies as to the true nature of Jesus' incarnation. It was specifically to die for the sake of Israel that Jesus had come.

It wouldn't be long before Jesus would be crucified, but until then Jesus stayed out of sight. This was His plan to lay down His life, not the Pharisees' plan to take it.

JOHN CHAPTER 12

BETHANY REVISITED
12:1-8

As you read the story of Mary and Jesus, think about how awkward this moment must have been for everyone at this dinner party. The smell of the perfume must have been overwhelming. The sight of another woman wiping Jesus' feet with her hair, and the thought of all that money poured out on someone's feet!

This was no ordinary dinner party, but then again, maybe the disciples were used to nothing being normal with Jesus. Luke tells us of another woman who had done almost the same thing in Galilee.

> *A woman in that town who lived a sinful life learned that Jesus was eating at the Pharisee's house, so she came there with an alabaster jar of perfume. As she stood behind him at his feet weeping, she began to wet his feet with her tears. Then she wiped them with her hair, kissed them and poured perfume on them.*
>
> *Luke 7:37-38*

JUDAS

There are two different story lines going on during this uncomfortable dinner party. First, John is going to give us a lot of information about Judas and what had been going on with him. John tells us that only Judas objected to the waste of this perfume, but the other gospels say that the other disciples joined in with his indignation.

The cost of this was immense. Many think that this was a dowry provided to Mary for her marriage. Because we are never told anything about their parents, some conclude that they had passed away and this store of perfume was a provision for them when they married. This was a luxury beyond imagination!

Jesus rebukes Judas and the rest who joined with him. He tells them that Mary had already decided to use the perfume on Jesus when He was buried, a testament to how deeply Jesus had affected her. Instead of waiting, something overcame her this day and she chose instead to anoint Jesus' feet with the oil.

Jesus made sure they understood He was not going to be around for much longer. This statement about the poor is not Jesus saying that we shouldn't try to supply for the poor or that there is no way to combat poverty, as many mistakenly use it to say. This is Jesus acknowledging a fact of life. People will always have situations that put them in poverty, but it is overwhelmingly clear that the Lord loves the poor. Jesus was only saying that He was more worthy of this gift than the poor because of who He was.

John takes this opportunity to let us see into Judas' character. Judas was the group's accountant and banker. He took care of all the money for Jesus and His disciples, but he was a thief and a liar. This second waste of expensive perfume that he could have stolen and spent on himself was too much for him. It won't be long before Judas' greed and sin would boil over in anger and rejection of Jesus.

One interesting paradox to consider is why Jesus would choose Judas knowing that he was going to steal from Him. Also, did John and the other disciples know all along that Judas was stealing, or did they figure it out afterward?

MARY

The other important aspect of this story is Mary. John passes over Mary because of what he is interested in moving the narrative of the plot to kill Jesus forward. Judas was integral to that, so he leaves out something important that Matthew and Mark point out.

> *Truly I tell you, wherever this gospel is preached throughout the world, what she has done will also be told, in memory of her.*

Matthew 26:13

This is no small thing. Again, John leaves this out on purpose because it detracts from the narrative of the plot against Jesus, but when we consider the harmony of the gospels, we see its importance. Jesus tells us that whenever the gospel is preached, Mary's story will be told.

Sometimes what looks like waste to us is of immense eternal value to God. Mary was not wasting this money, but performing an act that would be remembered for all human history and eternity as well. This was not waste, but an expression of extravagant love for God.

But why did Mary do this? Was she still overcome with the raising of her brother? Was she beginning to understand that Jesus had prophesied of His impending death? Was this the Lord who had prompted her to do such a thing? Maybe she had heard about the other woman in Luke 7 and she realized that this perfume she was saving should be used now.

Whatever the reason, her act is one of the most important acts of love toward Jesus in all the gospels and should not be overlooked.

THE PLOT
12:9-11

John gives us an ominous look into what is going on behind the scenes. Because Jesus had raised Lazarus from the dead, many people in Jerusalem were beginning to follow Him. Jesus had raised other people from the dead, but the fact that Lazarus had been dead four days and already laid in the tomb was beyond anyone's imagination.

It was because Bethany was so close to Jerusalem that made matters worse. Jerusalem was the center of the Jewish world, and it was where the Sanhedrin lived. When Jesus started to lead people away from them to follow Himself, that was when He crossed the line. Not only did they decide Jesus needed to die, but Lazarus as well.

How arrogant they must have been to think that they should kill a man that God had already raised from the dead! Not only that, but the fact that his name was Lazarus just like Jesus' parable that we have already looked at proves their blindness and rage.

BELIEF IN THE LIGHT
12:12-36

When Jesus decided to enter Jerusalem, the people there were waiting for His entry. They had heard about what He did for Lazarus and that He was back in Bethany and possibly would come to Jerusalem. They cried out to their savior, "Hosanna," even though they did not understand the method of His salvation. They were likely sure that Jesus was there to rescue them from Roman oppression. It wouldn't be long before they all turned on Him once they realized He had no intentions of freeing them from Roman rule.

Jesus rode into Jerusalem on a young donkey to fulfill the prophecy spoken of Him in Zechariah 9:9. John points out that none of them understood this at the time, but after Jesus was gone they had time to consider all these things.

Hindsight is always much better than what we perceive in the moment. The same was true for the disciples.

After Jesus had died, resurrected from the dead and then ascended into heaven, the disciples had time on their hands to try and figure all these things out. It is interesting that John points this out for us. The apostles were just people too, just as prone to not understand the gravity of the moments they were in until long afterward.

John tells us next that some Greeks had come to the festival. It is hard to know whether he means Greeks who had come to make money as merchants, or "God-fearing Greeks," a distinction we learn in Acts refers to Gentiles who worship Yahweh, but who never chose to become circumcised or follow all the Jewish customs. Regardless of who they are, it is interesting that Jesus seems to ignore them.

John tells us of many times when Jesus would say that His time "had not yet come." Now we see Jesus saying that His hour has come to be glorified. This introduces another powerful paradox of the gospel of John. Jesus is specifically speaking of being lifted up on the cross and dying when He uses the metaphor of a kernel of wheat. How is it that the cross is the glorification of Jesus? How is His graphic torture and death glory?

The cross of Jesus is perhaps the greatest mystery and paradox of the Christian faith. God shows His great love for us through death, and in that death He brings life. By laying down His life, Jesus glorifies the name and love of the Father, and in doing so the Father glorifies the name of Jesus.

After Jesus spoke of this paradox, God spoke aloud from heaven. This same crowd that heard the audible voice of

God the Father, who had just praised Jesus as He entered Jerusalem, would in just a few hours turn on Him and cry "crucify, crucify!"

Lest any man say that if only they could hear God or see God or touch God and they would believe, John offers us proof here to the contrary. These people saw God, they heard God, they touched God and then they crucified that same God.

When John tells us that some in the crowd said it thundered, he means that after Jesus had been crucified they had to change their testimony of this event, otherwise they would have to answer for their guilt. How often do men change the truth to fit the new sinful direction of their lives!

Jesus attested to the voice being for their benefit to approve of Jesus. It is obvious now that they understand Jesus' words about being lifted up meaning His death because they cite the belief that the Messiah would "remain forever," something that is true of the Messiah. They ask Jesus how He can be the Messiah if He isn't going to live forever.

Jesus doesn't directly answer their question. He tells them only to believe in the light while they still have it, meaning Himself, so that they can become sons and daughters of that light. John has hand-picked the works and words of Jesus that show that He is not a doctrine or a theology to be educated in, but a Man that we must know. Jesus did not want the people to know what He *meant*, but He wanted them to know *Him*.

BELIEF IN JESUS
12:37-50

We often take for granted the idea of belief in Jesus. It is tossed around in church from the time we are young. Here Jesus gives us His definition of what belief in Him looks like. John tells us that people saw the miracles Jesus performed, but refused to believe in Him. What does John mean, then, by belief, because these same people continued to follow Jesus around?

Jesus makes it very clear. Anyone who hears His words and keeps them, those are the ones who believe in Him. Those who hear and do not keep His words, they do not believe. That should give us pause to reflect on our lives, because Jesus Himself says that our relationship is tied not to just our affirmation of Jesus, but to our obeying what He says.

Jesus also reiterates this paradox of judgment. This time He says that He doesn't come to judge, but to save. He says that there is a judge for those who reject Him, specifically by not obeying them.

Herein we begin to understand the judgment Jesus speaks of. Regardless of who judges, the judgment is based on how we respond to Jesus' words. If we accept them and follow them, we will not be judged. Even if we accept them, but never follow them, it seems we will be subjected to this judgment.

John will delve deeper into this reality in the coming chapters, but this is a dramatically different idea than most often presented in churches. How can we reconcile it? How can we "accept" Jesus' words in the way He wants us to?

Don't forget to read John this week!
READ IT | KNOW IT | LIVE IT
For the word of God is living and active. Sharper than any double-edged sword, it penetrates even to dividing soul and spirit, joints and marrow; it judges the thoughts and attitudes of the heart. (Hebrews 4:12)

JOHN 13-14

STUDY QUESTIONS

1. Why did Peter refuse to have his feet washed by Jesus? Why did he then ask to have his entire body washed?

2. Do you think you would have been as confused as the disciples about everything Jesus said and did if you had been in their shoes?

3. Why is Jesus so troubled over His betrayal? Didn't He choose from the beginning for it to be this way?

4. Why do you think John wanted to be known as the disciple who had leaned against Jesus' chest? Why the disciple Jesus loved?

5. Why did Jesus prophesy to Peter that he would deny Him? Why three times?

How is Peter's betrayal of Jesus different from Judas'?

6. Why is Jesus preparing a place for us? Why is it better for Him to do that than to stay with us?

7. What does it mean to obey Jesus?

8. Why is it important to obey Jesus' teaching?

COMMENTARY NOTES

JOHN CHAPTER 13

THE EXAMPLE OF SERVICE
13:1-17

This is the account of the last supper held in the upper room of someone's volunteered space somewhere in Jerusalem. John foreshadows a little more about Judas as we begin the last supper encounter, but then quickly turns back to what Jesus' intentions are for the evening.

Jesus often did things that seemed strange and obscure to the disciples while they followed Him. We have to understand that all the gospels are written with a lot of hindsight and revelation of the Holy Spirit afterward, but that while these things happened that we read about, we must put ourselves in the shoes of the disciples and their comments.

Peter could not bear the thought of Jesus washing his feet. The conversation between Peter and Jesus seems a little absurd, because Peter had no clue what was about to happen. We know from Peter's actions in the coming hours that he still thought or hoped that Jesus was going to overthrow the government, or at least that he was going to prevent the rulers from taking Jesus without going through him.

Peter was trying to prove his loyalty, something at this point wasn't necessary. Jesus knew by revelation who was "His" and who wasn't. There wasn't anything Peter could do that Jesus didn't know, something that will become very obvious to Peter by the end of John's gospel.

Peter's original objection to Jesus washing his feet was immediately rebuffed by Jesus with harsh words so that Peter quickly changed his tone. I imagine John included this exchange because it must have been something they laughed about years later. Peter was nothing if not bold and persistent. Instead of resisting Jesus, he asked Him to wash his entire body.

Again Jesus responded by acknowledging He knew which ones of them were "His" and which one was not.

Jesus washed their feet to demonstrate something powerful to the disciples, something we need to examine today. He was modeling for them stooping down to serve them. He was washing their feet, something only a servant would normally do. That is why Peter initially rejected Jesus. He couldn't handle the idea of the Messiah acting like a servant.

Jesus did it specifically to place Himself in the role of a servant.

JUDAS AND JOHN THE BELOVED
13:18-30

Much like the Titanic has become a permanent metaphor, the name Judas is forever synonymous with betrayal. Jesus had hinted many times that He knew one of His disciples was "a devil," but He had never come out and said what He meant. Now, at this last supper, Jesus exposes what He has known all along.

Jesus plainly tells His disciples that one of them would betray Him. For once, Jesus is speaking very plainly, but it is such an incredulous word that no one can believe it or understand it. Why would anyone betray the Messiah? How could that even happen?

Jesus spoke plainly that He knew He would be betrayed, but then again chose to use a strange act to make known His betrayer. Why did He dip His bread together with Judas and then hand Judas His piece to show who His betrayer was? Why not just say it?

Whatever reasons Jesus had to expose Judas in this way, something else important is going on here with our author. At the same time Judas was giving himself completely to the works of Satan, John was running toward a completely new identity.

John pointed out that he, the disciple whom Jesus loved, was reclining against Jesus at the supper. What an odd picture for one of the "sons of thunder!" John, a rough and rowdy, macho fisherman, is leaning up against Jesus in front of all of his peers. The image that comes to mind seems more like a toddler leaning up against their beloved parent, and yet John owns it completely here. From here on, he wears this title with honor.

Something changed for John that night. When he calls himself "the disciple whom Jesus loved," he is not making a statement of Jesus' favoritism, but in the confidence he had in Jesus' love for Him. We know that God does not show favoritism (Romans 2:11), so what John means is that he had come to recognize that Jesus loved him. This confidence is something that we will see John express more in his gospel from here on.

Believing that God loves us is easy. Having confidence that He loves us and that we can reciprocate that love is hard. It doesn't come from Bible study. It doesn't come from having good theology (although bad theology can keep us from it). It comes from knowing God personally. When we have a relationship with Him, we can know Him and have confidence not only in His love for us, but also in our love for Him.

It is only in that place of reciprocal confident love can we truly grow in our relationship with Him.

John sandwiches this moment between he, Jesus and Peter in the middle of the revelation of Judas' intentions. It seems like Peter and John must have thought it was funny years later that in such a somber and tense moment, they were making faces at each other across the table to try and figure out who Jesus meant would betray Him.

For whatever reason, only Judas understands what is going on and Jesus willingly releases him to go and do what he has already planned to do. Other gospels tell us that at this very moment, Satan himself entered Judas. What a cataclysmic collision of the worlds of light and darkness!

PETER
13:31-38

Jesus tells His disciples that God and the Son are about to receive glory by Jesus' sacrifice. He encourages them that even though He will die and they cannot immediately follow Him to where He is going, that they are to love one another. It seems an odd thing to say in this setting.

Why would loving one another be a new command? Isn't God's love riddled throughout the Old Testament? Hadn't

Jesus taught love the entire time He was with them on earth? What did He mean a "new commandment?"

We will soon find out what kind of love Jesus means. It is not an average love, but a kind of love that outsiders will recognize His followers by. It is a love that will look like Jesus going to the cross for our sins.

Peter then asks Jesus why he cannot follow Him. Peter couldn't handle the idea of Jesus leaving or being taken away. Again, Peter announces his loyalty to Jesus in everyone's hearing that he would lay down his life to protect Jesus.

Jesus' answer was anything but predictable. He didn't thank Peter for his loyalty. He didn't acknowledge what a great help Peter had been during His time one earth. No, Jesus rebukes Peter.

Not only does Jesus rebuke Peter, but He rebukes him with a prophecy. Instead of Peter laying down his life for Jesus, Peter would deny that he even knew Jesus three separate times.

This prophetic rebuke must have stung when Peter heard it. He knew that he couldn't really argue with Jesus because he hadn't known Him to ever be wrong, but how could this be? How could he deny Jesus?

In a moment of incredible sadness, we will soon find out.

JOHN CHAPTER 14

By chapter 14, John shifts from Jesus' public ministry to His private teaching to the disciples. John 14-17 will be an extensive look at Jesus' private words to the disciples.

THE WAY
14:1-14

Jesus begins this teaching by telling the disciples not to lose heart. He knows that the first inclination they will have after He has died is to lose heart.

It is interesting that Jesus' comfort to them is that He reminds them that He has told them earlier that He would go away and prepare a place for them. We do not have this conversation recorded in scripture, but Jesus makes it clear why He will be going away and returning again.

John has taken great care to point out to his readers that Jesus was in fact the Messiah, but not as they had believed He would come. The Jewish understanding at the time is that the Messiah would come and make the Jewish state the seat of all power on earth and that Messiah would rule and reign from Jerusalem and bring all the earth under His dominion as a Jewish state.

This is a very accurate understanding of Old Testament prophecy, but incomplete. There are fewer, but very clear prophecies that the Messiah would "bear our sorrows" and come and be "cut off" and then return again (Isaiah 53:4 , Daniel 9:26).

John is making clear Jesus' messiahship and deity as an appendix to the common theology of the day.

The claim that Jesus is the "way the truth and the life" is one of the most famous passages and quotes by Jesus in the gospels. What we must understand about it is that Jesus' words were still unclear to the disciples when He said this. This was another obscure statement to them, so we should be careful not to commit it to our lexicon unless we understand what He meant by it.

He said that He was the "way to the Father." It is clear that He meant no one could get to, or truly know, the Father without knowing Jesus. Again, John does not want us to think that we can know about Jesus or be well-studied on the theology of Jesus, but we must know Jesus personally. Without an actual relationship to Jesus, we cannot know the Father. There is no eternal glory in the presence of God unless it is through a relationship to Jesus.

Jesus said that He was the truth. John has pointed out many times in his gospel that Jesus and the Father bear witness of His testimony. Having two or three witnesses was a reference to the courtroom, something the Sanhedrin had used as a principle of honoring each other to teach and lead. Jesus is calling Himself the truth as a reference to that courtroom of heaven. He is the true witness from God who testifies to what He has seen and heard in the heavenly places.

The fact that Jesus is "the light" is something that does not get fully explained in the gospel of John, but one of John's other writings explains it perfectly. Jesus wasn't being coy or cute when He said this. John tells us in Revelation that Jesus will in reality become the light that shines for all eternity. There will be no more sun, moon or stars to give light. Only God the Father and Jesus will illuminate all eternity.

In Physics, the universal constant, c, is the speed of light. It is actually the only constant in the universe, and it is the one that Jesus claimed that He in fact truly was. Time, space, distance and perception are all relative, but light is never relative. In the same way, Jesus is the way to the Father, the truth of who the Father is and the light of the Father. He is our universal constant.

Jesus told Philip that anything he wanted to ask, if he asked in Jesus' name, Jesus would do it for him. This is no small statement and one that has brought about great controversy through the years. Did Jesus literally mean "anything?"

THE HOLY SPIRIT
14:15-31

It seems like He did mean that, but not without a proper understanding of it. Jesus continued that thought by explaining that loving Him was synonymous with obeying His commands. Then He goes further and tells them that because they love Him, He will send them the Holy Spirit.

Jesus tells them that the "world," those who do not believe in Him in other words, will not accept the Spirit in the same way they would not accept Him. This concept of loving Jesus by keeping His commands and the empowering of the Holy Spirit are not divorced from the statement of asking for whatever we want, but are intrinsically linked together.

As with so many other things in his gospel, John makes it difficult for us to have wrong ideas about Jesus when we come face to face with His own words. Believing in Jesus to Him looks like obedience, not just a simple creed or a confession of faith. Those are important, but not enough, according to John 14 and 15.

Jesus again doubles down on this thought by reiterating that "Whoever has my commands and keeps them is the one who loves me." (John 14:21) That is unmistakably challenging to any thought of Jesus being some form of religion we can simply attend or hold as a belief on the side, unimportant to our normal lives. Love and obedience to Jesus are systematically tied to who we are and what we become.

When the other Judas asked why Jesus would not show Himself to the world, Jesus again speaks of obedience. Those who do not love Jesus will not obey His teaching and He will not show Himself to them and they cannot know the Father. Jesus even goes so far as to say that He doesn't say these things on His own, but that these words about obedience are directly from God the Father.

Jesus then says again that God will send the Holy Spirit who will be our advocate and our teacher. The Holy Spirit will be the one to remind us of Jesus' teachings. He will give us peace so that our hearts will not be troubled without the presence of Jesus.

THE PRINCE OF THIS WORLD

Jesus concludes His teaching to the disciples here by mentioning Satan, calling him the "prince of this world." Jesus says that his purpose is to show the world that Jesus loves the Father and does all that He commands. How interesting that Satan would show the world this.

God will use Satan's negative intentions to destroy the Son of God to display just how serious God's love is for us. In Satan's attempt to destroy God, he plays right into the strategy to redeem. Jesus is about to be faithful to His Father's will even to the death.

A horrifying death on one of the most heinous torture devices every constructed.

Don't forget to read John this week!
READ IT | KNOW IT | LIVE IT
For the word of God is living and active. Sharper than any double-edged sword, it penetrates even to dividing soul and spirit, joints and marrow; it judges the thoughts and attitudes of the heart. (Hebrews 4:12)

99

JOHN 15-16

STUDY QUESTIONS

1. What does it mean to bear fruit?

   What is the difference between pruning and cutting off?

2. What does it mean to be a friend of God?

3. Why will we be hated by the world just for following Jesus? What will that look like?

4. Why is it better for us to have the Holy Spirit than the physical presence of Jesus?

5. What causes people to reject Jesus?

6. Why is it so easy for us to self-justify ourselves?

Why is it important to reject self-justification?

7. Do you think you would have run like the disciples did? Why?

COMMENTARY NOTES

JOHN CHAPTER 15

REMAINING IN HIM
15:1-17

The first question that comes to mind as we read John 15 is, "what does it mean to produce fruit?" The language that Jesus uses here sounds especially harsh and seems to be more than just a gentle warning.

This passage gives us more questions than answers. True to form, John is not trying to help us learn more about Jesus, but to know Him personally. This is a challenging passage, and it takes knowing Jesus Himself to understand it. There are lots of different interpretations of this section, but the most important thing that Jesus says to His disciples is that they are already clean because they have the words He has spoken to them. He encourages them to "remain" in Him.

That is the comforting phrase here. Remember that Judas is no longer in their presence, so Jesus is making the distinction between the branches that will be cut off and those that will be pruned. Judas has been cut off, but the remaining eleven disciples are about to experience a pruning as they all run away from Jesus when He is arrested.

So then, what is the fruit that we must produce? The most obvious answer is that a grapevine produces grapes. If we are producing fruit, it would mean that we are reproducing who we are: making more followers of Jesus. Telling other people about Jesus and making new disciples, as Jesus will later command, is a primary task of all believers.

We also cannot divorce this passage from Paul's words about the "fruit of the Spirit."

> *But the fruit of the Spirit is love, joy, peace, forbearance, kindness, goodness, faithfulness, gentleness and self-control. Against such things there is no law.*
>
> *Galatians 5:22-23*

You could probably add to this a litany of things from throughout scripture, but the most important aspect here comes back to "remaining" in Jesus. That is the thing we will see Judas not doing, while all the other disciples will flee but quickly come back.

Do Jesus' words penetrate our hearts so that when we fall away (and we all do from time to time) we come back to Him, or stay away?

Jesus promises us that if we do remain in Him, we will bear fruit. That is comforting, but it still leaves us in tension with the idea of how do we "remain" in Him. What exactly does remaining mean?

Many people find Jesus' next words again disconcerting. He says that if we do remain in Him, we can ask anything we want and He will do it for us. That is not most people's experience with God, so this passage grows all the more challenging.

Have you experienced God giving you everything you ask for in Jesus' name? If not, why not? Is it because you do not remain in Him? Those are challenging questions that could leave us very unsure of our relationship with Him.

John is making sure we do not rest in a false hope of peace with God. This chapter is very challenging for us, and it calls for us to continue to grow closer to Jesus every day. Outside of a growing relationship with Him, we should not place our hope in anything else. With that said, does it mean that we are not "remaining" in Jesus if He doesn't answer our prayers? Not necessarily.

When Jesus was instructing His disciples to pray, He told them this parable in Luke 18:

> *Then Jesus told his disciples a parable to show them that they should always pray and not give up. He said: "In a certain town there was a judge who neither feared God nor cared what people thought. And there was a widow in that town who kept coming to him with the plea, 'Grant me justice against my adversary.'*
>
> *"For some time he refused. But finally he said to himself, 'Even though I don't fear God or care what people think, yet because this widow keeps bothering me, I will see that she gets justice, so that she won't eventually come and attack me!'"*
>
> *And the Lord said, "Listen to what the unjust judge says. And will not God bring about justice for his chosen ones, who cry out to him day and night? Will he keep putting them off? I tell you, he will see that they get justice, and quickly. However, when the Son of Man comes, will he find faith on the earth?"*
>
> *Luke 18:1-8*

Here Jesus is telling us that faith (remaining) in Him is not necessarily tied to our prayers, but our persistence in prayer. We should never think that because we pray something once, it will be done for us. We must persist. We must come boldly before God's throne and ask for what we want. If even a wicked earthly judge will act just to get this woman off his back, how much better is God to us whom He loves?

We cannot put our faith in a religious experience or set of rules, but in a relationship with the judge. We must never rest in growing in our love and affection for Jesus. That is how we remain in Him. That is how our prayers are answered. Jesus does not want us to learn about Him, He wants us to know Him.

Now Jesus shifts to teaching His disciples about love. Again, if we remain in Jesus, we will keep His commandments and we will learn to love one another. The joy that Jesus has to offer us is bound up in keeping His commandments.

Jesus reminds us that keeping His commandments, obedience to His words, is the way that we know we are in Him and we are His friends. We cannot ever forget that obedience to God is the way we show our love for Him.

When Jesus spoke of the parable of the talents in Matthew 25:14-30, He told the story of three servants. Two of them honored and loved the master and produced much gain for him. One servant, however, dishonored his master and disobeyed thinking him to be a wicked master.

The two loving servants who obeyed became more than servants. They were offered to enter into the "joy" of the master. That is the same joy that Jesus is speaking of here in John about obedience to His commands. In obedience to Jesus there is joy and love.

Most of the time we think of obedience as something we do begrudgingly for harsh parents, angry bosses and over-bearing spouses. Obedience to Jesus, however, is something that gives us life, liberty, joy and eternal life. It is not something we regret, but something that actually brings us joy!

Jesus is going to model that true love and joy by giving up His life to rescue us all from our sins. It is a love we only have once to give. No greater love can one have than this, and He has given it for us.

PERSECUTION
15:18-25

Continuing with the challenging words of John 15, Jesus now tells us that if we follow Him, other people will make life much more difficult for us. Persecution is now something we should expect, not something we should run from.

Jesus is not promising us that our entire lives will be nothing but persecution. What He is telling us is that we should not be surprised when it comes. Paul has this to say about persecution: If it is possible, as far as it depends on you, live at peace with everyone. (Romans 12:18) It is not always possible to live at peace with everyone around us, not because they do not like us but because they do not like Jesus.

John began his gospel by telling us that people rejected and hated the light because they loved their darkness. When people love their sin and wickedness more than they do the truth, they will naturally reject those who hold to the truth. When he wrote that it was a precursor for what Jesus is saying to us right now.

People do not reject Jesus for any other reason than they love their sin. They love darkness. Many people all over Israel saw the miraculous works Jesus did, but they chose to reject Him because they actually hated God. Their hearts were cold and bitter. Instead of dismissing Jesus, they actually persecuted and killed Jesus because He convicted them of their sin.

It would be foolish to go looking for persecution, but we must understand that if we remain in Jesus, persecution will find us from time to time. For many of us, it has a lot to do with our positions, geographic location and moment in history. The more people we interact with, the more we should expect to experience persecution.

Just by living our lives growing closer to God, we will inevitably convict others of their sin, which is something people hate. Conviction calls for change, and most people do not want to give up the sinful things in their lives.

THE HOLY SPIRIT
15:26-27

In light of certain persecution, Jesus again promises His disciples that the Holy Spirit of God will come on them and will testify to them about Jesus.

To end this passage of thought, Jesus reiterates the idea of fruitfulness. The disciples must testify about Jesus because they had been with Him. They knew Him. He did not want people who knew about Jesus to testify about Him. The Pharisees knew about Jesus, but they chose not to know Him.

Jesus does not want us to testify what we know about Jesus. We can only testify to the relationship that we have. How

107

often do pastors simply regurgitate the things they learn in seminary and people the things they hear from the pulpit in church? How often do people simply memorize and preach what they hear in Bible studies?

We must know Jesus. Apart from that, we do not have the testimony Jesus is after.

JOHN CHAPTER 16

MORE ON PERSECUTION
16:1-11

Thankfully, Jesus interrupted His warnings about persecution with the promise of the Holy Spirit. Knowing that the Holy Spirit will live inside us is comfort enough to face whatever may come our way, and Jesus gets back to telling us what that will be.

Rather counterintuitively, religious people are the ones who reject the truth most often. They have the most to lose from being wrong. Ministries, churches, Bible studies, book publishing houses, mission agencies and every other form of Christian outreach build their bases on a certain set of teachings or principles. If those are ever challenged by God or scripture, there is serious momentum to reject it.

What would happen if someone was shown to be wrong? What if a certain teaching many people put their hope in showed over time to produce little or bad fruit? It would be devastating to the power and money structure that had taken years and decades to build up.

Jesus tells the disciples that the persecution will come first from their own religious brothers. The fact that the disciples would be put out of the synagogue was a big deal, because it barred them from partaking in normal Jewish life.

The synagogue is more analogous to the place and role of the church in early American life than it is to the church in America today. Back then, the church was central to most things that happened in a community whether you were a devout Christian or not. It was the center of community. In the same way, being put out of the synagogue meant that Jews would lose their community. Longstanding friendships, business opportunities and family tensions would be the result of being put out of the synagogue.

Jesus then goes and says something rather bombastic. He tells His disciples that religious people will think they are doing God a favor by killing them. Remember that this will be rather obvious after they have their way with Jesus shortly, but at this moment this must have been a ridiculous statement to the disciples. How could any religious person want to kill someone else to do God a favor?

Never underestimate the human condition under sin. Bitterness, anger and violence are always under the surface when sin reigns in someone's life. The fact that most people do not act on that violence has more to do with cultural and societal pressures than with the violence itself.

When Hitler began exterminating Jews in Germany, he did not do it alone. He had thousands of willing volunteers among the German military and civility. He could not have killed millions without civilians and soldiers alike being so willing to kill. The problem was not that Hitler made them all worse than they would have been otherwise, but that he provided them a socially acceptable outlet for the violence already in their hearts.

In Jewish life, there was a socially acceptable outlet for such violence in strict conflict with the Word of God. Think of how often men picked up stones to kill Jesus with on the spot. They were very quick to exact justice themselves when they felt like someone had blasphemed God. How often today do we see those who say "peace and love" turn violent in their speech when they get offended or things do not go their way? What lurks inside the heart of man is universal apart from the intervention of the Holy Spirit.

> *The heart is deceitful above all things and beyond cure. Who can understand it?*
>
> *Jeremiah 17:9*

MORE ON THE HOLY SPIRIT
16:12-15

Jesus could have told them more about what was coming, but He knew that they could not bear it. Jesus again shifts back to the Holy Spirit. It is a lot to think about suffering under the hand of wicked men without understanding that we have an advocate. We have One that will teach us, guide us and speak to us everything He sees the Father doing just as Jesus did.

CLEAR SPEAKING
16:16-33

Jesus had just given the disciples an ear full about persecution, the Holy Spirit and many things that were to come, but when He said they would not see Him anymore "in a little while," they were confused about what He meant. They started whispering among themselves. This must have seemed a little strange to Jesus because this isn't a large group. Instead of waiting for the disciples to get up enough courage to ask, Jesus preempts them.

Through more figurative language, Jesus explains that He will die and that most people will be glad at His death. As His disciples are mourning, they will receive the Holy Spirit and then one day in the future they will be reconciled to Jesus in eternity.

At this point the disciples probably did not understand all of what Jesus was telling them, but in doing so He finally acknowledged that He had been speaking in figurative language. When Jesus told them that He was about to stop speaking figurative and begin speaking clearly, you can almost feel the joy that overcame His disciples. Just by telling them that He was going to stop speaking figuratively, they announce that He must be from God.

This is a testament to just how difficult it was to be in Jesus' company during the past three years. Here are the men who had seen everything Jesus had done for years, and just now do they have confidence in Him simply because He promised to speak clearly from then on.

This was probably a little bit of hyperbole on the part of the disciples. They had seen the miracles. They had heard Jesus explain clearly all the parables He had told. He gave them clear and inside information He didn't give to everyone else. But still, they struggled with Jesus speaking figuratively.

The disciples did not understand everything Jesus had said, but they knew Him. Jesus made it intentionally difficult to understand what He was saying without actually knowing Him.

Jesus finishes this moment of wonderful epiphany for the disciples with a downer of a word. He tells them that they will soon be "scattered." To their ears, this must have sounded reminiscent of all the battles that Israel had lost in its history. The phrase, every man being scattered and returning to their homes was what would happen when Israel would face an unexpected defeat before the enemy.

Jesus was telling them in advance that they would suffer this terrible tragedy, but that it was okay. It was ordained by God to happen that way, even though it would be devastating to each of their hearts.

The idea that life in Christ is always ever increasing and ever more prosperous is not a biblical idea. God certainly does love it when we prosper and when we grow, but He will never give us more at the expense of us growing through His purposes. This moment of defeat was ordained so that His disciples would learn to trust in the Holy Spirit once their Messiah was cut off.

Even though it would seem in the moment like the world had overcome their Messiah, Jesus promised them it was not as it would seem to be. He would actually overcome the world through His death, not the other way around.

When it seems the world comes crashing down around us, it is not always as it seems. Remember that in the moment of greatest distress among the disciples, Jesus' comfort to them was that He had overcome the world!

Don't forget to read John this week!
READ IT | KNOW IT | LIVE IT
For the word of God is living and active. Sharper than any double-edged sword, it penetrates even to dividing soul and spirit, joints and marrow; it judges the thoughts and attitudes of the heart. (Hebrews 4:12)

JOHN 17-19

STUDY QUESTIONS

1. Why does Jesus pray for the glory He once had before the creation of the world?

2. Why did Judas come with a mob?

3. When Jesus said, "I Am He," what did He mean? Why did the men fall down backwards?

4. Why did Peter deny Jesus after knowing that Jesus told him he would do it?

Do you think you would have done the same thing in the same situation?

5. Why did the Jewish leaders hand Jesus over to Pilate? Why didn't they just try, convict and kill Him themselves?

6. Why did Pilate have Jesus flogged? Why do you think he had Jesus crucified if there was nothing He did deserving of death?

7. Why does Jesus command John to take care of His mother?

8. What did Joseph and Nicodemus give up by handling the body of Jesus? Would you have made a similar sacrifice if you were in their shoes?

COMMENTARY NOTES

JOHN CHAPTER 17

JESUS PRAYS FOR GLORY
17:1-5

This chapter is a long prayer of Jesus John has recorded for us. This is one of the most beautiful chapters in John because Jesus not only prays for Himself, for His disciples, but also for those of us reading these words nearly two thousand years later.

When Jesus prays for His glory, He does not take it for Himself, but asks the Father for it so that He can in turn glorify the Father with it.

What is beautiful here is that Jesus asks for a restoration of the glory He had before He left heaven to put on human flesh. What the disciples had seen of Jesus was a masking of Jesus' true glory while on earth. At the mount of transfiguration, three of His disciples were allowed to see but a glimpse of Jesus' true glory, but now Jesus is about to re-enter His true glory.

JESUS PRAYS FOR HIS DISCIPLES
17:6-19

Jesus continues a prayer that seems to be as much a message as a prayer. The words He is saying is like a conversation between He and His Father that He wants everyone else to understand.

Jesus' mission while on earth was not to raise up an army of believers in Himself or in God. No, Jesus had a laser-focused mission of claiming the very few from just the nation of Israel that were His. It would become the disciples' job, and subsequently our role, to bring in the harvest of souls into the kingdom of God.

That glory would come to Jesus through His disciples is a truly amazing concept. That means that we today bring in the glory of the earth that belongs to Jesus. It is the right and responsibility of every believer since these disciples to gather in the glory of Jesus on earth.

It reminds us of the story of the first missionaries of the Moravian Brethren. A group of disaffected Christians in the middle of 17th century conflict in Europe had begun a prayer meeting that would go on to last one hundred years without ever stopping. 24 hours a day, 7 days a week for one hundred years their prayer meeting lasted.

Not too long after it began, the Moravians began to be stirred to reclaim this glory that belonged to Jesus in the earth. In a somber moment, the group heard a story from some runaway slaves that there was an island in the New World where the slave master would not allow any Christians. He wanted no testimony of Jesus there for fear the slaves would become filled with hope.

Two young men were moved so deeply by the need for a Christian witness on this island that they willingly sold themselves into slavery on this island. Many from the group went to the port to see them off as they made the harrowing journey across the ocean, never to be seen or heard from again. As the boat launched, one of those on the shore called out through their tears, "Why?! Why are you doing this?!"

"May the Lamb who was slain receive the rewards of His suffering!" They shouted back, their last words to those they knew on earth.

The glory that Jesus will receive from us on earth is the growth and multiplication of His followers on earth. Jesus did not raise up a large group for Himself. In fact, by all measures, Jesus was a terrible failure at building a kingdom. It is a testimony to the power of God through the leadership of the Holy Spirit that there are Christians on every continent now, separated by centuries, languages and thousands of miles from this small group overhearing this prayer.

Jesus prayed that God would protect His disciples through the power of the Father's name. He prayed that His disciples, including us today, would have the "full measure" of His joy. The joy of the Lord is nothing to take for granted. We should constantly be asking the Lord to give us this "full measure" of His joy. We need it because of the reality Jesus would reveal next.

Jesus acknowledged that the world was going to hate His disciples because of God's word they had received. John was very intentional in the opening of his book to mention that the world hated Jesus, the Light, because it loved darkness. Every bit of light that exposes the darkness of the world causes a terrible reaction of hate, anger and bitterness.

Jesus did not want them, nor us today, to be protected from the world by being removed from the world, but to be protected from the plans of our enemy, Satan, and his kingdom of darkness. That Jesus asked for God to sanctify us, or to continually purify us from the means and methods of sin deep in our hearts, is challenging.

It is obvious then that the indwelling of the Holy Spirit is not enough for us, but that the ever-increasing exposure of light to shine on the darkness of our hearts is necessary for us to grow in God. Just like Jeremiah said that our hearts are wicked and deceitful, we must never assume that we have overcome the world as Jesus has because we have the Holy Spirit. We must continue to grow in our love for God or we will grow cold. Sanctification is the necessary thing to protect us from the plans of the evil one for us.

JESUS PRAYS FOR HIS DISCIPLES' DISCIPLES
17:20-26

When Jesus thought about us today, the "ones" who would believe through the message of the disciples, He was interested in one primary thing. He wanted us to be "one," just as He and the Father were one. That Jesus would ask for a level of unity between believers that He and His Father shared together is almost scandalous!

How is it possible for Christians to be so bound in love and unity for one another that we would enjoy the same level of fellowship that God and Jesus enjoy with one another? Yet that is exactly what Jesus prays for when thinking of all the believers throughout history.

It is through this unity that Jesus says the world will recognize Him. Think about that! The miracles of Jesus were not enough to convince the cold, dead hearts of the Pharisees and Jewish leadership that He was actually from God, but the unity of the believers that would follow would be! We know this isn't just theory, but it actually happened.

In Acts 7, we see that when there was a division between the Christians in Jerusalem, the apostles appointed elders to help govern the disputes. When those disputes were put to rest and unity restored, even the Levitical priests began joining the Christians. We know that not long after that the Pharisees began joining them.

That unity among believers is a more powerful testimony to Jesus than miracles is an amazing idea, but it is exactly what Jesus is saying here, and it is the very thing throughout the centuries that has sparked some of the greatest awakenings in history.

Jesus concludes His prayer for all the believers that would follow by asking for the love that flows between He and the Father would flow in us as well. Again, what a scandalous idea! How could humans contain the level of love that God has for us? How can we know that love and express that love for others?

That is exactly what Jesus prayed for us, and it is exactly what we should continue to pray for today, that this prayer would be fulfilled in us. Lord, make us one as You are one, and fill us with the same love You have!

JOHN CHAPTER 18

JUDAS BETRAYS JESUS
18:1-5

The fact that the darkest moment in history followed one of the greatest revelations and prayers in history is no mistake on John's part. The darkness that is quickly rising and about to strike in Jesus' life is not surprising to Him, but all part of His ordained plan.

Jesus is going to allow the darkness that is lurking in these evil men's hearts to fully come to light by them carrying it out. Virtual bitterness, anger, hatred and violence is about to become real. Jesus is not going to be overcome by darkness, but He is going to reveal it!

This is not a story of Jesus being taken by surprise. Jesus went to the very place He knew Judas would come looking for Him. Judas had with him a detachment of soldiers and officials of the chief priest of Israel, who would have been allowed to have such protection under the governing Roman authorities.

It seems surprising that the guards brought weapons. Jesus even asks them in Matthew why they came with weapons (Matthew 26:55). Keep in mind, though, how deeply the Jewish leadership misunderstood Jesus. Remember that He was the same man who, on several occasions, rather violently wrecked the Temple courts where money changers and merchants were.

Jesus had been available for them to arrest at any time publicly. They chose to arrest Him at night so that the same people who had welcomed Him as king when He entered Jerusalem just hours before would not turn on the Jewish leadership. They did it secretly at night so they could get away with their evil plans.

I AM
18:5-6

One of the most powerful moments in revealed human history was to happen this night on the Mount of Olives. When they told Jesus that they were looking for Jesus of Nazareth, He gave them a very interesting response.

When Moses sat before the burning bush, he asked the One speaking to him from within the flame who He was; who was Moses to tell the Israelites who sent him.

The voice of God from within the bush said this:

> God said to Moses, "I AM WHO I AM. This is what you are to say to the Israelites: 'I AM has sent me to you.'"

> Exodus 3:14

There are many names that God is referred to by in the Bible, but only one name that He refers to Himself by; "I Am."

When Jesus responded with His true name, the name that He had from eternity past and will hold for eternity to come, all the men there to arrest Him fell down backwards. The power of His true name literally knocked them over. This moment was one of the greatest revelations of who Jesus really was, but it also was one of infinite kindness.

We do not know exactly how all creation came to be other than that God spoke and it all existed. Scientists claim that there as a cataclysmic event which they call the "Big Bang." It was when all matter and all energy that exists in the universe sprang into being from some unknown source. We know that source. John tells us at the beginning of this gospel that it was the voice of Jesus Himself.

This same breath that gave birth to all the unthinkably infinite energy that our universe contains is the same one that gently knocked these men over when He revealed His name to them. That all the universe did not explode in the same cataclysmic event that birthed it when the Son of God, our Creator, uttered His name while being arrested for simply revealing Himself to those wicked enough to arrest Him is a kindness we will never fully understand.

JESUS ARRESTED
18:7-14

Jesus pressed the issue again and the men foolishly continued their cause. It is amazing that energy all these men simultaneously felt did not persuade them to change course.

Jesus told the men to let all His disciples go and to only take Him. It would seem that they came with this intention to completely quell whatever they thought Jesus was planning to do. Peter confirmed their fears when he swung his sword at one of the guards and narrowly missed killing him, only cutting off his ear.

For whatever reason, John leaves out the part where Jesus picks up the man's ear and puts it back on his head and restoring him to his previous state. His rebuke of Peter must have been a devastating blow to all the disciples; that there would be no fight to protect Jesus. They were going to have to simply watch as their Messiah was carried off by wicked men with wicked intentions.

PETER DENIES JESUS
18:15-18

How quickly Peter's world turned upside down! He was literally willing to kill for Jesus and just moments later he was going to fulfill Jesus' prophecy about denying Him. We cannot judge Peter too harshly here; we may not have fared nearly as well as he did.

We must also not assume that Peter's denials here are simply out of fear. Moments before, Peter was willing to go to battle for Jesus. It would seem more appropriate for Peter's actions to be primarily from a place of hurt and betrayal. Peter believed Jesus to be the Messiah, yet here He was being carried away a prisoner. Everything Peter had believed was coming crashing down in a matter of moments.

Remember that Jewish understanding of the Messiah had nothing to do with a suffering servant dying for our sins. The Messiah to them was only a man who was going to restore all the earth to God through Israel's rulership in Jerusalem. Peter still had not understood the full measure of who Jesus was.

JESUS' MOCK TRIAL
18:19-24

It was not technically legal for Jesus' trial to take place at night, but it is totally fitting with the revelation of darkness Jesus was making known in all these men's hearts.

Jesus plainly answered the high priest about His teaching, that everything He had said was public. It is also clear here that the high priest wanted Jesus' disciples arrested too.

Annas and Caiaphas were related through marriage. We know that there was some political jockeying and monkeying that Herod and the Romans had done with the position of high priest during this time. Generally, the high priest was appointed for life to sit in the seat of Moses as the 71st person on the Sanhedrin. Annas and Caiaphas had been switched in their position, presumably for a sense of loyalty to the Romans.

Annas chose instead of continuing his questioning of Jesus to send Him on to the current high pries, Caiaphas, his son-in-law.

PETER FULFILLS JESUS' PROPHECY
18:25-27

John now jumps back to Peter and shows us that Jesus' words came to pass exactly as He had told Peter. Three denials and a rooster crowed. It wasn't until this moment that Peter realized what had happened. Luke gives us a little more detail about this moment:

> *The Lord turned and looked straight at Peter. Then Peter remembered the word the Lord had spoken to him: "Before the rooster crows today, you will disown me three times."*

Luke 22:61

This was a devastating moment to Peter, where the frailty of his heart was revealed to him. The weight of this must have been unbearable. We know that Peter went away and "wept bitterly" after this moment (Luke 22:62).

MORE OF JESUS' MOCK TRIALS
18:28-40

By the way that Pilate responds to the angry Jewish mob of leaders, it does not seem like Jesus is their first victim. This seems to be something he is used to dealing with when it comes to them.

When Pilate asked them what charges they were bringing against Jesus, they couldn't give him a straight answer. Pilate had heard this song and dance before, so he tried to send them away. By saying that they had no right to execute anyone, they were not being completely honest. It was true that under Roman rule they were not allowed to execute, but these same men had already picked up stones before to kill Jesus with. If they had wanted to kill Him themselves, they would have done so already.

What the Jewish leaders wanted was something altogether different. Caiaphas had already told these men that Jesus must die as a sacrifice to save all Israel. What he meant was that he wanted to turn Jesus over to Pilate and say Jesus was trying to overthrow the government claiming to be the rightful ruler. He was trying to show loyalty to the Romans so that the constant uprisings and terrorism that Jewish zealots were carrying out was not something they were behind.

The Jewish leaders were worried that the Romans were going to crack down on them and remove all leadership by the Sanhedrin. History tells us that Israel was a very dangerous place to live at this time. There was constant terrorism by the zealots to try and make the Romans give up the land as too difficult to manage.

The Sanhedrin was turning Jesus over to Pilate because they wanted Him to die a slow, painful and embarrassing death. They thought that if He was crucified that everything He stood for would quickly die off with Him.

Crucifixion was something so repugnant to people of that day, there is actually very little written about it. It was a death reserved for only the worst of the worst, and the Jews were going to insist on it to squash everything that Jesus was.

Or so they thought.

Pilate wanted to know if Jesus thought that He was a king. Jesus equated His kingship with truth, something He knew would catch Pilate's attention. We have more detailed accounts from the other gospels of Jesus' interaction with Pilate. From all four gospels we find that Pilate actually became afraid of Jesus because something was very different about Him.

Jesus wasn't afraid of Pilate. He didn't beg for His life. He spoke to Pilate as someone with authority. Pilate had never encountered that. Even Pilate's wife had a dream about Jesus the night before and she warned him not to have anything to do with this business.

Pilate tried desperately several times to release Jesus. He even asked them if they wanted him to pardon Jesus and instead they asked for a terrorist to be pardoned. This revealed their true intention.

If they had wanted to prove their loyalty to Rome by turning in someone who was trying to overthrow the government, why would they then ask that Pilate release someone who had actually already tried to do it? No, this was jealousy, murder and rage in their hearts, pure and simple.

JOHN CHAPTER 19

A BRUISED REED
19:1-16

Pilate had Jesus flogged, thinking that would be enough to satisfy the blood lust of the Jews. He underestimated their hatred and jealousy.

Flogging was not just a lashing with a whip, but more than likely with a "cat of nine tails." It was a whip with many ends with bits of jagged pottery and glass embedded in it. It was intended not just to cut like a whip, but to drag the skin and rip flesh out with each blow. By the time they put the crown of thorns on Jesus, He was a bloody, unrecognizable mess.

Instead of taking pity on Him in this state, the Jews shouted Pilate down to crucify Jesus. This was their only intent from the beginning.

When Pilate heard that Jesus called Himself the Son of God, it terrified Pilate. He had never met a man who spoke to Him like Jesus, and now he thought that he may be standing before a god.

Jesus chose to speak very little to Pilate, and only to let Him know that He was the one who had given Pilate his authority in the first place.

Isaiah had seen this when the Lord showed him a vision of the Messiah.

> *He shall not cry, nor lift up, nor cause his voice to be heard in the street. A bruised reed shall he not break, and the smoking flax shall he not quench.*
>
> *Isaiah 42:2-3*

What a sad moment when the Jews cried out that they had no king besides Caesar. Instead of accepting their true Messiah, the very One they had been waiting for, they begged their oppressors to have Him put to death.

JESUS' CRUCIFIXION
19:17-27

Pilate sent Jesus on to be crucified, but not without further mocking the Jews. He put a sign on top of Jesus' cross so that all those people from out of town for the Passover could read that Jesus was their king. This enraged the Jewish leaders. They wanted Pilate to write on it that Jesus had only claimed to be their king, but that He really wasn't.

The Lord's plans will always be fulfilled. When He has prophets and people willing to walk with Him, He will use them to carry out His plans. When people reject God, He will still use them to carry out His prophetic plan. We see that here. Caiaphas had prophesied, unknowingly, that Jesus must die for them. Pilate rightly called Jesus their king. Even the wicked Roman soldiers unwittingly fulfilled prophecy by casting lots for Jesus' undergarment, as prophesied in Psalm 22.

John tells us that he, three Marys and Jesus' aunt were there watching all this. Jesus looked down at Mary and John and commanded the one disciple who had quickly come back to His side to take care of His mother. From that day on Mary would live with John. History tells us that John ended up in Ephesus and that Mary moved there with him, where she died. What an amazing responsibility and privilege!

JESUS' DEATH AND BURIAL
19:28-42

John gives us a very short account of Jesus' crucifixion, unlike the other gospel writers. He was the only one of them who was an eye witness to the event. It is telling that he only tells us that it happened but gives little detail. It must have been a horrible memory for John to watch Jesus suffer and die there. How awful to have to sit there with His mother and not be able to offer any consolation.

Jesus' life was not taken from Him. He gave it up willingly, and He even chose the moment of His death. He offered up His spirit and left His body.

John lets us know that the guard who pierced Jesus' side to see if He was dead later became a Christian. He would later go on to testify that Jesus' legs were not broken and that he indeed had pierced His side just as the prophet had foretold in Psalm 34 and Zechariah 12.

Joseph of Arimathea and Nicodemus took the lifeless body of Jesus and prepared it for burial. Both these men were on the Sanhedrin, and in doing this they probably ensured that they would no longer be. What they gave up they gained back billions of times over.

What a wonderful honor and privilege to be the ones that God tasked with handling the dead body of Jesus. Jesus was dead for less than 72 hours, and these two men were the only men who handled him. For all eternity, Jesus' body was without life for this short period, and Nicodemus and Joseph were the only ones to care for that body.

They placed Him in a new tomb that had no other bodies in it. They did not know it at the time, but this would prove to be very important. There would be no denying that it was Jesus who had come to life, because He was the only one laid in the tomb.

Don't forget to read John this week!
READ IT | KNOW IT | LIVE IT

For the word of God is living and active. Sharper than any double-edged sword, it penetrates even to dividing soul and spirit, joints and marrow; it judges the thoughts and attitudes of the heart. (Hebrews 4:12)

JOHN 20-21

STUDY QUESTIONS

1. Why does John tell us that he outran Peter?

2. Why didn't Mary understand that Jesus had risen from the dead? Do you think you would have made that connection?

3. Did the disciples receive the Holy Spirit when Jesus told them to, or did they receive it on the day of Pentecost? Is there one moment when we receive the Holy Spirit, or more than one?

4. Why wouldn't Thomas believe Jesus had risen from the dead without feeling His hands and side? Was he wrong for doing this?

5. What is the main reason John wrote his gospel?

6. What did the Jews think the Messiah was supposed to do? What do you think the Messiah is supposed to do?

7. Why did Jesus ask Peter three times if he loved Him?

8. Why does John want us to wrestle with the paradoxes he introduces in his gospel?

COMMENTARY NOTES

JOHN CHAPTER 20

JOHN RUNS FASTER
20:1-10

John's continual reference to himself as the "disciple Jesus loved" is a beautifully coy device. It shows the real human interaction with the divine in writing this gospel. It displays the real emotional connection John had with Jesus while playfully referring to himself as the one that Jesus really loved. It is like John is poking fun at the other disciples by saying, "I don't know about you, but I know He loves me. Maybe He loves you too, but I can't be sure. What I do know is that He loves me." It is easy to imagine lots of laughter at the dinner table with the other disciples in Jerusalem in years to come as John referred to Himself in this way.

When Mary found the tomb empty on the day after Passover, two days after Jesus had been laid in it, she decided to go and get Peter and John for help. She wanted them to help find Jesus' body, not an explanation of what had happened to Him.

Just like his coy reference to himself, it seems that John enjoyed including little tidbits about his experiences that would playfully get under the skin of the other disciples, especially Peter. Here he makes sure the reader knows that it was him, and not Peter, who arrived at the tomb first. He does give Peter credit for stepping into the tomb first, though.

John does tell us conclusively that they did not yet understand that Jesus was alive, but only that He had been moved. This was probably a horrible exclamation mark on what had been a tragic weekend. Jesus was dead and now even His body was missing. What else was there for them?

MARY MAGDALENE
20:11-18

Mary Magdalene went back to the tomb after Peter and John and stayed there crying. She was terribly bothered by the fact that someone had so obviously stolen Jesus' body. The fact that Mary knew the two men in the tomb were angels and was not afraid at their presence, as is so often the case in scripture, may give us insight into how great her grief was.

When Jesus, the presumed gardener spoke to Mary, she continued in her grief-stricken pity. But then Jesus did something amazing. It was something that would stay with Mary the rest of her life. It is something that has rung clear from this gospel for centuries and it will be the thing that impacts us the most deeply for all eternity.

Jesus said her name.

In saying her name, Mary was instantly released from the fog of grief and sadness that had covered her and her eyes were immediately enlightened to what was going on. The doctrinal realization of Jesus' sacrificial atonement for our sins with His blood will never lose its power, but it can become easily sanitized by familiarity. One thing that never seems to become too familiar is the realization that God knows our name. When He speaks our name, the truth of His sacrifice, His devotion, His caring and His love come instantly rushing over us.

Mary felt all that in a moment and she was undone. When she heard her name, she immediately knew who she was talking to. Hearing her name spoken by her risen savior immediately changed her for all eternity.

What came next is still one of the greatest mysteries in scripture, though. What exactly Jesus meant by this statement is something that we may only have answered for us when we ourselves meet Him face to face. What did it mean that she could not hold on to Him because He had not ascended to the Father? Was He speaking of literally touching Him? Did He mean that He was not going to be around for very long, so she needed to go back with the believers and learn to trust the coming Holy Spirit?

Whatever the meaning, she was obedient. She left His glorious presence to testify to the disciples that she had seen the risen Jesus.

THE DISCIPLES AND THOMAS
20:19-29

The disciples had gathered to figure out what was going on. It was now a day and a half since Mary had told them that she had seen the risen Jesus, but He had not appeared to them. They were also rightly terrified of the Jewish leadership, because it was not Jesus alone who the guards had come looking for with Judas. They were there to arrest them as well, and it was only Jesus' command and authority that prevented that from happening. Now that He was gone, they probably feared the Jewish leaders would finish the job if they had the chance.

How Jesus got through the door, or wall, or window that evening is a mystery. The nature of His, and our coming resurrected bodies, is a mystery to our human minds today.

Jesus seems to effortlessly move around, hidden or disguised, and then appear inside locked rooms. Coupled with stories like that of Philip in Acts 8 being supernaturally transported across Israel lead us to believe that eternity with Jesus will be very amazing indeed.

Jesus offered the disciples in this impromptu meeting the opportunity to receive the Holy Spirit. Again, what exactly He meant is a mystery. Was this a prophetic promise of what was to come in a few weeks, or was this the moment that the Holy Spirit began to indwell them?

Not only does Jesus raise more questions than answers with His proclamation of the Holy Spirit, but with His next statement He grants uncommon authority to mankind. When the Pharisees confronted Jesus over forgiving of sins, they rightly said that only God could forgive sins, not realizing who they were speaking to. Now here we find that Jesus, God made flesh, is granting the delegated authority to do the very thing that only God can do. This is a huge blessing and a weighty authority all at once.

Jesus takes very seriously the authority He has given us with our speech. When we choose to follow Him, He not only grants us salvation from a future of unspeakable torment, but He offers us unthinkable authority. We must be very careful with our words, because in them we hold tremendous delegated authority given directly from our Creator Himself.

> But I tell you that everyone will have to give account on the day of judgment for every empty word they have spoken.
>
> Matthew 12:36

> *The tongue has the power of life and death, and those who love it will eat its fruit.*
>
> *Proverbs 18:21*

Solomon knew this all too well when He proclaimed this. This authority was nothing new to mankind, but now it was codified in eternal law by Jesus Himself. It is not only weighty, it is powerful. It is supernatural. We see it on display as Stephen begs the Lord's forgiveness upon his assassins for ignorance of what they were really doing, just as Jesus had also done (Acts 7:60).

John next tells us about Thomas and his absence from their first meeting with Jesus. Thomas has been the butt of reproach through Christian history for his doubt that Jesus was alive, but he actually gives us a perfect view into human nature. It was not the evidence of God coming into contact with mankind that caused the unbelievers to believe in Jesus. The Pharisees saw His works, but refused to believe.

Thomas assured the disciples nothing would make him believe Jesus was alive except that he felt the scars in Jesus' hands and side for himself. It wasn't the evidence that eventually convinced Thomas to believe. It was the intimate presence of Jesus. Perhaps Thomas actually put his hands in Jesus' side, but John tells us that it was when Thomas saw Jesus that he believed.

Evidence did not change Thomas, the Presence did. Evidence may count for something, but it will never supersede the need for the very Presence of God in our lives.

Jesus promised Thomas he was blessed for believing, but He promised even greater blessing for those of us who never experienced the evidence, but only the Presence.

JOHN'S PURPOSE
20:30-31

At this point, the book of John abruptly changes, and John seems to conclude his gospel. He tells us the explicit purpose for this work, bookending the stories contained within with a reiteration of the initial chapter.

All this was to show conclusively that Jesus was the Messiah. John's aim was to explain that the Messiah and God's Son were one and the same. All Old Testament scripture pointed to this very fact, but John chose not to provide us with a proof text of that. Instead, he introduced us to the Messiah Himself. He did not want us to academically know that Jesus was the Messiah, he wanted us to believe He was the Messiah so that we may have eternal life.

JOHN CHAPTER 21

Some scholars believe that John concluded his gospel with what is now chapter twenty and that this chapter is a post-script added by the elders of Ephesus. If that is the case, this chapter was very likely something John recounted to them over and over again. If it was added, it was certainly something that John would have given them at least tacit approval to include in his old age. It speaks to events that were many years in the future to come. Whether it was added by others or not, it bears the mark of John's continuing testimony nonetheless.

CATCHING FISH
21:1-14

During His resurrected period, Jesus seemed to be transitioning the disciples to life without His direct presence. The fact that Jesus seems to appear to the disciples so little in the forty days He walked the earth is mysterious. Here we find the disciples relocated to Galilee from Jerusalem. Perhaps they had been too afraid of the Jewish leaders to stick around and found their home base a safer place.

John then tells us a second story of a miraculous catch of fish. The first is recorded in the Gospel of Luke:

> One day as Jesus was standing by the Lake of Gennesaret, the people were crowding around him and listening to the word of God. He saw at the water's edge two boats, left there by the fishermen, who were washing their nets. He got into one of the boats, the one belonging to Simon, and asked him to put out a little from shore. Then he sat down and taught the people from the boat.
>
> When he had finished speaking, he said to Simon, "Put out into deep water, and let down the nets for a catch."
>
> Simon answered, "Master, we've worked hard all night and haven't caught anything. But because you say so, I will let down the nets."
>
> When they had done so, they caught such a large number of fish that their nets began to break. So they signaled their partners in the other boat to come and help them, and they came and filled both boats so full that they began to sink.

When Simon Peter saw this, he fell at Jesus' knees and said, "Go away from me, Lord; I am a sinful man!" For he and all his companions were astonished at the catch of fish they had taken, and so were James and John, the sons of Zebedee, Simon's partners.

Then Jesus said to Simon, "Don't be afraid; from now on you will fish for people." So they pulled their boats up on shore, left everything and followed him.

Luke 5:1-11

Even though John never tells us this initial story, he seems to allude to the fact that we should already know it. This was the moment that Peter initially believed in Jesus, and Jesus would use an almost identical experience to call Peter back to Himself after his painful denial.

DO YOU LOVE ME?
21:15-17

After they had all eaten the fish that they caught, Jesus looked at Peter and asked him a question three times. There are not too many places in scripture where we need to study Greek or Hebrew to understand the Words contained, but this is indeed one of them. Our English does not contain the proper connotation of the word translated "love" to adequately understand what Jesus was saying. It is not so much a translation problem as much as it is a cultural difference.

The Greeks had many different words for which we now translate them all as "love." When Jesus asks Peter three times if he loved Him, he does not use the same word. The first two times Jesus uses the word "ἀγαπᾷς," or agape. It carries the connotation in English that we most often define as "unconditional love," or the love one would have for a child or family member.

The third time Jesus asks the question He used a different word entirely. He asked Peter if he "φιλεῖς" Him, or if he had "phileo" love for Jesus. This is most often understood in English as a brotherly love, or a tender affection. It implies a less rigid love bound by familial relationships and instead one of chosen affection.

This was no slip of the tongue by Jesus. By all accounts, we see that Peter not only denied Jesus three times, but that on the third time he was quizzed whether or not he knew Jesus, He "called down curses and he swore to them, 'I don't know the man!'" (Matthew 26:74)

Jesus asked Peter three times if he loved Jesus to correlate to Peter's three denials. The third time He used a different word to correspond to Peter's over-the-top denial the third time. The response to each of the three questions was the same for Peter, though: "feed my sheep."

Jesus was not only telling Peter that he was forgiven, but that he had responsibility. Jesus has not saved us from our sins, even the most egregious of them, to languish in a type of purgatory, removed from purpose. No, He has saved us from our sins to a life of eternal purpose that we must choose to walk into. Peter had to overcome the guilt of his failing and choose to walk into his calling, just as we do today.

One thing Peter said was telling, though. Peter's confidence in his love for Jesus is amazing. He had learned through three years of relationship that nothing could be hidden from Jesus. He knew he could not lie here. That he had as much confidence in his love for Jesus after his denial is amazing.

Oh, that we could only have the same confidence in our love for God! So often it is not our confidence, or lack thereof, in God's love for us that is our undoing, but confidence in our love for Him. We may know that God loves us, but we stumble when we question the genuine nature of our love for Him. Our adversary constantly accuses us of being disingenuous in our love for Him to our great peril.

Through all the friendly ribbing he gives Peter, John marvels here at Peter's amazing character. Peter, for all his flaws, is the one disciple who had superior confidence in his love for Jesus. John may have called himself the "disciple Jesus loved," but Peter was henceforth defined as the disciple who knew he loved Jesus.

RUMORS OF JOHN'S DEATH ARE GREATLY EXAGGERATED
21:18-24

John rounds out this amazing story with a rather strange one. As soon as Jesus had finished telling Peter to feed the sheep He would provide to him, He prophesied of Peter's death. This may not seem like a kind word at the tail end of Jesus' recommissioning of Peter, but it was kindness indeed. When we have to endure great difficulties, knowing in advance can be of great comfort.

Jesus was, in essence, telling Peter he would die on a cross one day, and Peter understood that. We know from church history that Peter did die on a cross in Rome under emperor Nero's wickedness.

John includes Peter's response as the final gesture of playfulness in his gospel. Peter, unsatisfied with how this moment had turned, looked at John and asked Jesus what was going to happen to him.

Jesus told Peter that it was not his concern. The phrase He used was interesting, and one that John now has to clarify. Jesus told Peter that he had to follow Him regardless of what happened to anyone else. He said that if he wanted John to remain alive until He returned, it was not Peter's concern.

That little phrase would come up years later, and is most likely the reason John tells us this story.

We know from historical accounts that John was the last of the apostles of the Lamb to die, and the only one not to die a martyr.

The story goes that John had been living in Ephesus and that the church was continuing to grow, much to the chagrin of the locals, as we see when we read about Paul's experience there in Acts 19. The people decided to execute John for his treason against their customs by burning his flesh off his body while still alive, a most gruesome death. They put John in a human-sized vat of boiling oil. The problem was that it did not kill John.

There must have been a very awkward moment for the officials who placed John in that boiling oil when they realized it wasn't killing him. Church history tells us it did not even hurt him. Imagine that moment, standing there, looking at the man you were supposed to be executing with horrendous pain, simply staring back at you as if you were both standing in a security line at an airport!

After this encounter, the people were afraid of John and decided that they should exile him to the remote island of Patmos instead of trying to kill him. That is the place John was when he wrote the book of Revelation.

John makes the point through all this that Jesus did not say he was not going to die. John did one day die, just not as a martyr, but as an old man. John was putting to rest the rumor that he would never die that obviously circulated through the church when they heard of these events. He was saying that it was not a promise to him, but only a direction to Peter that he should only concern himself with his own destiny.

As should we today.

ALL THE BOOKS IN THE WORLD
21:25

John concludes his book with one final acknowledgment. Jesus did so many more things than what he had recorded for us to know about. John was laser-focused on his goal of convincing us Jesus was the Messiah. He included few stories even the other gospel writers did, but seems to reference to them. They did not serve his purpose. His only purpose was to convince us Jesus was God Himself and for us to know Him personally.

John concludes with the fact that Jesus did so much, that it will take an eternity to discover all He actually did while He was here on earth.

And for those of us who believe, that is exactly what we will have.

Don't forget to read John this week!
READ IT | KNOW IT | LIVE IT
For the word of God is living and active. Sharper than any double-edged sword, it penetrates even to dividing soul and spirit, joints and marrow; it judges the thoughts and attitudes of the heart. (Hebrews 4:12)

READING CHART

WEEK 1
- ☐ Day 1: Chapters 1-3
- ☐ Day 2: Chapters 4-7
- ☐ Day 3: Chapters 8-10
- ☐ Day 4: Chapters 11-14
- ☐ Day 5: Chapters 15-17
- ☐ Day 6: Chapters 18-21

WEEK 2
- ☐ Day 1: Chapters 1-3
- ☐ Day 2: Chapters 4-7
- ☐ Day 3: Chapters 8-10
- ☐ Day 4: Chapters 11-14
- ☐ Day 5: Chapters 15-17
- ☐ Day 6: Chapters 18-21

WEEK 3
- ☐ Day 1: Chapters 1-3
- ☐ Day 2: Chapters 4-7
- ☐ Day 3: Chapters 8-10
- ☐ Day 4: Chapters 11-14
- ☐ Day 5: Chapters 15-17
- ☐ Day 6: Chapters 18-21

WEEK 4
- ☐ Day 1: Chapters 1-3
- ☐ Day 2: Chapters 4-7
- ☐ Day 3: Chapters 8-10
- ☐ Day 4: Chapters 11-14
- ☐ Day 5: Chapters 15-17
- ☐ Day 6: Chapters 18-21

WEEK 5
- ☐ Day 1: Chapters 1-3
- ☐ Day 2: Chapters 4-7
- ☐ Day 3: Chapters 8-10
- ☐ Day 4: Chapters 11-14
- ☐ Day 5: Chapters 15-17
- ☐ Day 6: Chapters 18-21

WEEK 6
- ☐ Day 1: Chapters 1-3
- ☐ Day 2: Chapters 4-7
- ☐ Day 3: Chapters 8-10
- ☐ Day 4: Chapters 11-14
- ☐ Day 5: Chapters 15-17
- ☐ Day 6: Chapters 18-21

WEEK 7
- ☐ Day 1: Chapters 1-3
- ☐ Day 2: Chapters 4-7
- ☐ Day 3: Chapters 8-10
- ☐ Day 4: Chapters 11-14
- ☐ Day 5: Chapters 15-17
- ☐ Day 6: Chapters 18-21

WEEK 8
- ☐ Day 1: Chapters 1-3
- ☐ Day 2: Chapters 4-7
- ☐ Day 3: Chapters 8-10
- ☐ Day 4: Chapters 11-14
- ☐ Day 5: Chapters 15-17
- ☐ Day 6: Chapters 18-21

WEEK 9
- ☐ Day 1: Chapters 1-3
- ☐ Day 2: Chapters 4-7
- ☐ Day 3: Chapters 8-10
- ☐ Day 4: Chapters 11-14
- ☐ Day 5: Chapters 15-17
- ☐ Day 6: Chapters 18-21

WEEK 10
- ☐ Day 1: Chapters 1-3
- ☐ Day 2: Chapters 4-7
- ☐ Day 3: Chapters 8-10
- ☐ Day 4: Chapters 11-14
- ☐ Day 5: Chapters 15-17
- ☐ Day 6: Chapters 18-21

ABOUT THE AUTHOR

Darren Hibbs is the founder of the 10 Week Bible Study. He believes that the methodology of studying the Bible in this book can radically transform your life with God.

By filling your heart and mind with the Word of God first and foremost, you will better know God's heart than if your Bible knowledge comes primarily from sermons or even the commentary provided within this book. There is nothing more powerful for transformation than a people who know for themselves the Word of God.

Darren's heart burns to bring a message of hope to a lost and broken world through the immeasurable love of Jesus. It is his heart that the church will grow in love for God and embrace His love and power so that the lost will see and hear the good news about Jesus as they see it change us.

Darren writes regularly and can be reached at www.DarrenHibbs.com.

OTHER TITLES BY 10 WEEK BOOKS

The Year of the Lord's Favor? Two days before 9/11, an angel visited Darren in a dream and showed him the collapse of the World Trade Center. In another dream in 2003, the Lord showed Darren that in the days when the replacement building, One World Trade, was complete, America would hang in the balance.

Find out how these remarkable prophecies came true and what it means to you today.

Revelation: A 10 Week Bible Study is a different kind of Bible Study that will take you deep into the scriptures and cause you to engage God's Word like never before.

With helpful commentary and probing questions, the 10 Week Bible study will help you find a new love for God's Word. Ten weeks really can change your life!

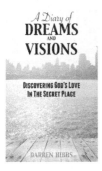

A Diary of Dreams and Visions is a book designed to encourage your faith to ask big things from God. Through engaging stories, Darren Hibbs shares several short stories of how God spoke and moved prophetically. This book will encourage you to ask things of God you never thought to ask before!

AVAILABLE AT AMAZON.COM TODAY

Made in the USA
Monee, IL
06 April 2021